CANNIBAL

*The True Autobiography of a White Man
in the South Seas*

by

WILLIAM DIAPEA

*printed from the manuscript
in the possession of*
THE REV. JAMES HADFIELD

with a foreword by
H. DE VERE STACPOOLE

G. P. PUTNAM'S SONS
NEW YORK — LONDON
The Knickerbocker Press
1928

FOREWORD

WILLIAM DIAPEA, known as Cannibal Jack, inquiring of his own soul the reason of his wanderings, received no very definite reply. Pleasure perhaps; perhaps to chase shadows or to escape from himself; perhaps just for the joy of being alive.

Whatever his reason he was surely, and out of his own saying, the king of all wanderers and worthy of the kingdom he had chosen—the Great Pacific Ocean.

They say the moon left the bed of the Pacific and went as a vagabond into space; if so she left in her bed something of her dreams and main desire, for of all the places in the world here is the home of unrest; of the desire to keep moving coupled with the objects and means of locomotion. Trade winds, currents, beckoning islands, the call of pearls, of copra, of bêche-de-mer, or phosphates and, in the old days, of sandal wood and black birding, all these were and are part of the conspiracy between the something restless and obscure in man and the great blue sea that brings the blown-away canoe to help in the mixing of the Island races and the Japanese swordfish on the *Kiro Shiwo* current to the Californian Coast by way of Alaska!

But the Pacific is the home of laziness as well as of unrest—and when were the two ever entirely separated? Never in my experience in the case of odd jobbing, beach-combing, petty trading wanderers such as William Diapea—unless in his case—for I know of no record such as he indicates, and I believe with truth. "In fifty years," says he, "I have visited almost everything in the way of islands situated on that vast expanse of ocean bounded on the north by California, Japan, China and India, and on the south by Tasmania, New Zealand and Australia, and everything included between the west coast of South America and New Guinea and Papua."

Following all sorts of trades and avocations, from musket-mending to pig-breeding, he reckoned that he had touched at more than a thousand islands and resided on nearly a hundred. He admits quite openly that he had been a hard-shell polygamist, and a hard drinker, and the reputation of being the father of

FOREWORD

38 children and the grandfather of 99 sits quite easily upon him—at least he does not try to tear it off, but rather crowns himself with the fanciful notion that if this reputation be founded on fact he may yet be the great-grandfather of 999 or 1,000 great-grandchildren.

Drinking, trading, fighting, musket-mending, pig-breeding, procreating his species and frying in the sun, one might imagine that this amazing specimen of the White Races would have had his time fully occupied. Not a bit. He tells us himself that he had been writing for forty years before at the age of seventy he presented this precious volume to Mr. Hadfield, the well-known missionary. And on page 88 he gives us to understand that the present narrative formed only a part of a much larger autobiography "written in nineteen common copybooks," of which we have here only the contents of three. If the other sixteen copybooks had anything of the texture of these three their loss surely leaves the literature of High Adventure for ever the poorer.

Mr. Hadfield and the Publishers are to be congratulated on their rare good taste in preserving the original manuscript from the touch of any "literary" hand. A page here and there may be cloudy, but any cloudiness is not of style but of speech; for Cannibal Jack does not write, he talks: he button-holes you, he belches in your face; when he has done, it is not the end of a book, but the stopping of a voice; the end of an evening, the end of a bottle of whisky; with a plate full of cigarette ashes on the table and the tropic dawn standing at the door.

How much truth has he told? How much truth has he hidden? Did he ever meet Litia? Did he ever try cannibalism as some people try caviare for the first time? I cannot say, but if he never met Ratu Finau—read the extraordinary account of that gentleman running from page 112 to page 121—then he had a power for character invention denied to most novelists, and if he never went whaling he yet managed to forestall one of Bullen's most striking observations on the habits of whaling ships.

For my own part this book goes upon the shelf beside Aloysius Horn's *Ivory Coast in the Earlies* and Melville's *Typee,* feeling sure, as I do, that neither Horn nor the author of *Omoo* would turn up their noses at the company of William Diapea.

H. DE VERE STACPOOLE.

INTRODUCTION

M Y first and only meeting with Cannibal Jack
was about the year 1889, when I had occasion
to pay a visit to the Island of Maré, which lies about
40 miles south-east of Lifu where I lived at the time.
You may find the respective positions of these two
islands by following Latitude 22 in a map of the
South Pacific from West to East as far as the
French penal settlement of New Caledonia. Adjacent to this, and on the East side, you will find the
Loyalty group of islands, consisting of Maré, Lifu
and Uvea, and governed by the French as dependen-
cies. Continuing to follow this same latitude, but
slightly more to the North, you will arrive at the
groups of which Cannibal Jack has most to say in
the present volume, namely the Fijian and the
Friendly groups.

It was—as already said—on the Island of Maré
that I met Cannibal Jack. I had paid several visits
to the island in past years, and no one could wish for

a heartier greeting than I received on landing, both from chiefs and their subjects—a race of sturdy men and handsome women. The chief boast of this island is that neither its present occupants nor their ancestors have tasted the flesh of white men. Many of the Maréites could speak the language of Lifu, and in conversation with a party of these I was told that a very old man had recently landed on the island, that he was a stranger to everybody except the very old men; and that he was staying with my old friend Dirty Jerry, the beach-comber, doctor and storekeeper of the district. The next day I received a call from this new arrival. Old he certainly was and grey-bearded, though still lithe and unbent by age. His deeply furrowed face, while indicating past hardships and anxiety, bore also an expression of shrewd intelligence, tempered by an amiable and friendly smile. Altogether—despite his old and frayed apparel—he was a man of distinguished bearing. To make a general comparison of his appearance with one well known to us all, I would invite the reader to think of Mr. Bernard Shaw.

As he entered my room he introduced himself as William Diapea, telling me he had heard of my arrival, and had called to pay his respects. I suspected later, however, that the true object of his visit was to obtain a stock of writing-paper. I was glad to be able to supply this want in the shape of a few exercise books, for which he was undeniably grateful.

I do not remember much of our conversation, but his personality made a deep impression on my mind. I was surprised to learn during our talk that he spoke the Maré language (which I did not speak), also the three languages of the other two islands of the group (of which I spoke only two). I gathered also that Mr. Diapea was in low water as regards funds, and I was pleased to be of service to him in giving him a few light articles of clothing. I have no doubt that it was in thankful recognition of this that he asked me to accept an exercise book closely filled with an account of some years of his adventurous life. This account is now presented just as it left the hands of Cannibal Jack, excepting one incident mentioned by him which the most friendly censor would hardly have passed. I could not find an opportunity of reading the manuscript at the time, but later when I had leisure, I took it up more from curiosity than from any expectation of pleasure. Although the handwriting was most trying and indistinct, I found I must finish it before laying it down. I was charmed, and at times thrilled, as I accompanied Cannibal Jack from island to island. My regret on closing the book was that the writer had used such coarse language and described events in so realistic a manner as to preclude any thought of publication. (It should be remembered that we were then in the Victorian epoch.) I therefore stowed the MS. away with other derelict material, where it would have remained in obscurity or have been destroyed had it not been unearthed and perused by one of my sons who reads every scrap of South Sea literature he can lay his hands on, and who clamoured for its immediate publication.

At the time of my interview with the author, I could not be expected to know what manner of man he might be in private life. It was not till later that I learned the nickname by which he was known in the islands of the South Pacific. He was said to have deserted as a boy from a vessel which called for provisions at the Island of Maré, and on which he was serving an early apprenticeship. Outward appearances are not to be relied on, as I had already discovered during the nine years I had then spent at Uvea and Lifu. A very entertaining work might be written on the South Sea Island traders. They can

INTRODUCTION

hardly be said to form a type, so far as my experience goes. Some are men of exemplary character, others are the opposite. You may meet with one who is as wise as a college professor, and another as ignorant as a country yokel. One needs to be prepared for surprises. I once had a French convict living next door to me, and found him to be not only sincere and honest, but excellent company, and I may truthfully add that I never had a neighbour who had not some attractive quality of heart or mind. One reason for the strange companionships of dwellers in these islands is perhaps that they are reduced to Hobson's choice. Even Dirty Jerry, who was proud of his first name and endeavoured to live up to it, was as popular as anyone in the entire group; and I am sure Cannibal Jack, during his stay at Maré, found him a kind and most entertaining host, though he might have wished that the adjectival prefix of his name had not so fittingly qualified his dwelling. Poor Jerry! One wonders what his old friend and schoolfellow, the New South Wales Australian Prime Minister at that period, would have thought at the sight of this long-bearded, grimy old beach-comber, who had no use for toilet soap and made it widely known that he took a severe

xiii

cold whenever he washed his face, and who managed to keep immune from colds by avoiding water to the end. Nevertheless he was a jolly good fellow.

I have met other traders in the South Seas, who, with a little training and suitable environment, would, in my opinion, have become illustrious statesmen or judges. One man with whom I was brought into close contact was endowed with such a gift of fabrication that no one who knew him gave credence to any statement he made. What a loss was here to the world of fiction and light literature! Hayes was the name of this man (not the world-famed Bully Hayes of an earlier date) and he was one of the cleverest raconteurs I have ever met. He had heaps of stories in his repertoire, chiefly of whaling expeditions and cannibal feasts which he had attended. On one occasion he told me of a visit he paid to one of the big chiefs of Lifu, who invited him to stay to dinner. As he (Hayes) sat by the open door he saw a native attendant rush from the Chief's house after a boy who chanced to be passing, whom he clubbed to death, and who subsequently formed a part of their repast. Hayes protested that he declined that loathsome dish, but it was commonly believed that he had often indulged in cannibalism. His denial is not to be wondered at, for the practice is to-day in such evil repute that no native ever cares to speak or think of it. I knew of only one exception to this rule, namely an old village chief who was accustomed to gloat over the superior flavour of roasted human breast over that of fowl or pig.

In this story Diapea denies cannibalistic practices. I trust that I am not traducing his name if I suggest that in spite of this disclaimer it was the accepted opinion in the Islands that he had been addicted, as no doubt were not a few white men, to such practices; nor is it an unkindness to suggest that this disclaimer may have perhaps been actuated by the sincere regrets of an old man. That he had such regrets for some of his past deeds is clearly manifested in these pages.

Several of the white settlers of early days who were in the Loyalty Group before I arrived in 1878 are said to have been cannibals. However, I should much prefer to give them, as well as Cannibal Jack himself, the benefit of the doubt. He admits much, but not cannibalism.

Some may wonder that a missionary should assist in the broadcasting of Cannibal Jack's occasional disparaging and even hostile criticisms of missionaries. When we reflect, however, how frequently (though it may be reluctantly) he pays tribute to their beneficent labours, we feel we can well afford to let him have his say, and even to take counsel from his more sagacious strictures. We cannot, of course, expect glowing testimonials from men whose mode of life is quite at variance with our teaching. Nevertheless such testimonials are constantly being given. Even Cannibal Jack contributes his quota. Moreover, his book will serve an excellent purpose in revealing—as in a cinema—the conditions of native life before the arrival of the missionary.

It appears to me that every clean-living English-man who sees for himself the difficulties, obstacles and achievements of this work must, and usually does, become a more or less ardent supporter of a cause which has done so much for the social, mental and spiritual benefit of these savage islanders; and incidentally for the material advantage of the civil-ized world.

In conclusion I may add that I have complete con-fidence in the veracity of Cannibal Jack. Much as his story is reminiscent of Robinson Crusoe, he did not appear to me to be a member of the school of romanticists. His range of experience was so wide that he had no need to draw on his imagination, as did Defoe. I doubt if his adventures were ever questioned by his contemporaries, unless perhaps when he disclaimed the distinction of being Cannibal Jack in word *and* deed. Certainly I have discovered little or nothing in his book inconsistent with what I have learned during more than forty years of service in the South Seas.

J. HADFIELD.

PUBLISHERS' NOTE

This letter of Mr. Read's disposes of the hope hitherto entertained by Mr. Hadfield and the publishers that the rest of Cannibal Jack's Autobiography might be discovered.

many years ago, back in 1860, I think, was earnestly
desired by the French on north end of New Caledonia, for murder and selling arms and ammunition
to revolting natives. If he had been caught it was
the first wall and a firing squad, but he and others
stole a small craft and went to Fiji. That is all I
know. He was what old Artimus Ward called the
Kangaroo, 'an amoosin cuss.'" (It will be noted
that Mr. Read spells Cannibal Jack's name Diaper;
but the name in the MS. from which this book is
printed is clearly Diapea.)

Mr. Hadfield, in a letter to his son, Dr. J. A.
Hadfield, comments as follows:—

"Evidently he [Mr. Read] knows little more of
Cannibal Jack's history than we do; at least little
that will be of any use to us. I remember Streeter's
arrival from Fiji in the stolen cutter, but did not
know that Cannibal Jack landed at Luengöne at the
same time. The cutter was named *The Stranger,*
and by the way, you, with the rest of us made a trip
in her to Uvea. I remember this owing to the
smallness of her bulwarks which necessitated the
tying of one of you to each of my arms for safety
during the night. I don't expect any help from Tib
Hagen after learning from Read of the destruction
by fire of J. Robertson's house."

PUBLISHERS' NOTE

POSTSCRIPT

SINCE the Introduction was written and set up in type Mr. Hadfield has received from Mr. J. F. Read, a trader living in Lifu with whom he has maintained a regular correspondence, a letter containing the following additional information relating to Cannibal Jack:

"You ask about the late Mr. John Diaper, alias Cannibal Jack, alias Silver Eyes. He died at Maré years ago in the savour of Sanctity aged about 80 or 82. He did leave some papers as he had the mania for scribbling. These papers, on death of Dirty Jerry Imber, passed into possession of Robertson Imber and went to glory at the late fire. This son calls himself John Robertson. I only saw Cannibal Jack at the time he ran away from Fiji with old Streeter. Streeter ran away because he had to, and Jack also was 'wanted.' You may remember that they landed at Luengöne, chez Forrest, who promptly swindled them out of all cash, goods and also boat, made a slave of Streeter, who was a boozer and would give his soul for a nip, or if no nip was to be had, a bottle of Pain Killer. Diaper was not to be bounced, he had nothing and so emigrated to Maré to live with Dirty Jerry. Diaper

PUBLISHERS' NOTE

EXCEPT that the spelling of place-names has been standardized for the reader's convenience, the spelling, punctuation and paragraphing in the narrative which follows are those of the author. It has been thought better to leave even slips of the pen untouched, for these slips are often characteristic of the writer. For example, *hoc omnus geni* still stands on page 38, though on page 85 he gets the phrase right. The only liberty taken with the text has been the omission of two passages. The first of these follows the second line on page 9; it is the equivalent of two pages in the present volume, and deals, in a manner at once tedious and inaccurate, with the Fiji language. The second is the passage referred to by Mr. Hadfield as too questionable to print; it is indicated by asterisks on page 221, and is the equivalent of four pages in length. The section numbers on pages 9, 89 and 144 appear in the original MS.

A FEW EXTRACTS
FROM THE
AUTOBIOGRAPHY OF

WILLIAM DIAPEA
ALIAS "CANNIBAL JACK"

[THESE EXTRACTS EMBRACE
THE LONG GONE-BY YEARS OF
1843 UP TO 1847—THE LAST
INCLUSIVE]

I SUPPOSE the reader will expect an explanation of how I, in the first place, came in possession of the somewhat disgraceful-sounding sobriquet of "Cannibal Jack," and which I have since taken as my *nom de plume.*

Well then, as it is now a long time ago since I first commenced scribbling—some forty years—and among the rest, I named one book *Jack the Cannibal Killer,* thinking perhaps, as everything is in a name, that it would have the greater circulation, but instead of remaining at that, it was, by some means or other, altered, and "Cannibal Jack" became indelibly fixed upon myself. And, besides, as I told a Mr. M., manager of a sugar mill on the R. estate, Fiji, when he asked me, "How in the name of goodness I ever became the owner of such a name?", that the nincompoop portion of the community, when they learned that I had been such a great number of years among cannibals, naturally concluded (I being in such a very small minority among them), measuring my corn by their bushel, that I had become one myself! He (Mr. M.) also told me that I must have imbibed a great many of their evil practices, and, no doubt, he included cannibalism!

I told him that that supposition, no doubt, held good with inferior men, when he said, "Then you imply that you are yourself a superior one," and then I told him that he alone must be behind the times, because all the world, himself excepted, knew that!

I was in search of an overseer's situation on the estate. He asked me what I expected a month, when I told him that I had received sixteen pounds a month at the same employment in the last place I occupied. He said he could get *young* men for six! I told him, I hoped he did not compare young men to myself! He said, of course not, "because they can do much more work than you can!" I told him that I never did *any* work, because by so doing I should lose prestige in the eyes of the Fijians; and when I ordered them to hurry along with their work, they would tell me to do it myself, seeing I was a working man like themselves! A very great difference between this gentleman and Mr. E., Manager of the Deumbea Estate, because I only asked twelve pounds a month from him, and he paid me at the rate of sixteen, and yet he belonged to that part of the "land *of Cakes*" where it is said that a Jew cannot by any possibility make a living! He was an Aberdonian, but then he was a man of experience and not a new chum, and a perfect gentleman besides! I don't know what part of the same country Mr. M. belonged to, and I don't very much care!

THE following pages are extracts taken, almost at random, from the autobiography of William Diapea, *alias* "Cannibal Jack." I have been wandering now for upwards of fifty years—in fact it may be said sixty, including the truant days from school, whilst in England. I have visited almost everything in the shape of islands situated in that vast expanse of ocean, bounded on the north by California, Japan, China and India; and on the south by Tasmania, New Zealand and Australia. And also everything included between the west coast of South America, i.e. Peru and Chili, east, and New Guinea or Papua, west. And, to make a long story short, I have touched at a great many more than 1,000 islands, and resided on nearly 100. I have been in all the above-mentioned countries, and continued to exist, after a fashion, for a short time, at every imaginable occupation, by land and water, going to them in vessels of various sizes and different nationalities; as for the islands, they, a great many of them, have been visited in small schooners, cutters, and boats, sometimes my own, oftener other people's, and, in canoes, I have also made trips of hundreds of miles, nay, thousands, putting all the trips together!

My acquaintances, who, by the by, seem to know as much of my antecedents as I do myself, have long since declared that I am the reputed father of 38 children, and 99 grandchildren, and so, that being the case, I shall in a very few years more be the great-grandfather of 999—perhaps 1,000—great-grandchildren, and if I live long enough for this to become a *fait accompli*—and I don't see why I should not, seeing I have observed through an already longish life—now my seventieth year—that a great many people, when overtaken by what I should call *little* ailments, generally die, and that just because they think they are going to, and are also afraid that they shall! which has not hitherto been my case. I say, that when the above becomes a *fait accompli,* I think

6

I shall then be entitled to gratulate myself on not having lived or written in vain.

I T may be inquired "what I was endeavouring to accomplish by these erratic movements of mine." Well then, the answer is, that I did not then know any more than I do now, excepting, perhaps, that I might have been running round the world for sport, or, better still, that I was—like thousands of others before me, thousands of years ago, as well as now, at this present time, and will be for thousands of years to come, if the world stands long enough—trying to run away from myself, or chasing shadows,—these latter, of course, I did not catch, and the former fear I did not realize; but I was like an Irish shipmate of mine on board a tyrannical Yankee whaler, when the skin and grief "Old Man" asked him "what he was grinning at," conceiving, in the smallness of his pinched soul, that he had no business to look pleasant, but Pat told him that he was laughing because he was alive! And so, in like manner, if I enjoyed myself as I went along, I don't know whose business it is, excepting my own!

With respect to the American whaling fleet—and it well deserved that appellation if only in reference to the number, for there were 500 sail out of the port of New Bedford, to say nothing of other parts, which contributed to their quantum also. It was in a succession of these ships that I saw what is never seen in any other trader on the water, for they creep and slide into the most outlandish holes and corners of the world, where other ships are afraid to go on account of not being so well able to defend themselves against savages on account of the paucity of their crews; and besides, there is nothing in those kind of places worth going for, excepting by these whale ships, which go principally to replenish their stock of fresh provisions, which can be obtained at a nominal price, as well as their wood and water; and another item in the desideratum is that there are no white authorities—hardly a Consul—to ask the "Old Man" unpleasant questions regarding the usage he has generally given his crew!

I had forsworn whaling, as I thought, for life—never having been particularly fond of the business in itself—but, after being clear of it a score of years, I was again obliged to have recourse to this somewhat distasteful pursuit, in order to extricate myself from some of these same places, which I had so imprudently thrown myself into!

No. 9

WHILST I was enjoying myself as best I could, eating and drinking—drinking the "yagone" in unlimited quantities and bidding fair to become quite a sot, like the rest of the whites in other parts of Fiji, the principal portion of them being located in a settlement called Levuka situated on the island of Ovalau (Central Fiji or "Lomai Viti"),—I say, whilst I was doing all these things, alternated by mending muskets and amassing property, and living quite content with my three wives, one morning, or rather perhaps in the middle of the night, as it could not have been much past twelve o'clock, if any, Bonavidogo came along, rousing me up from a sound sleep, telling me to buckle on my cartridge box, and which, by the by, contained sixty rounds of cartridges, shoulder my musket, and also not to forget my dirk or sheath knife, and follow him, for the enemy were astir, and "Bakolas" were to be had just for the killing of them. I followed quite drowsily, not being more than half awake, through the effect of the beastly habit I had lately given way to, of imbibing the juice of that very lethargic root, and besides, I followed reluctantly enough, because I was not at all interested in their murderous kinds of warfare, not caring two pins which side beat, as neither party had, at present, injured me, but still I followed in silence, as all the natives maintained the strictest silence, as is their wont when on the war-path.

We followed down the path of the hill, leaving Naviu behind, and got on to the plains and made for the salt water and into the canoes, made sail, and sailed along down the coast with a fair wind, keeping generally about two miles from the shore, sometimes three. Just as daylight began to break there was an island ahead of us. We kept that island between us and the main. It appears that some of the natives in our canoes had descried a number of small canoes pushing off, or already off the shore of the main, and were paddling towards this low island, which was full of coco-nut trees, and were coming here for the purpose of getting coco-nuts to make sennet [1] from their husks, as well as for the purpose also of eating the meats—a thing they had been accus-

[1] A kind of flat braided cord made of coco-nut husk fibre.

tomed to do all their life, as well perhaps their fathers before them, and which our people, it seems, were aware of, and had come purposely to catch them and cut them off, and that was the reason they had started on this bloody expedition in the night, and had kept the island between us and the main as well as between their intended victims' canoes and ourselves, so that our canoes should not be seen by these poor doomed creatures. It appears also that our canoes had not been seen by these unfortunate fellows. Our canoes just reached the shore of one side the island, as the fleet of the *enemies*' canoes, as they would and did call them, landed on the other side. Nearly all our people landed, excepting a few which were left in each canoe, to pole them round inshore by water to the fleet of the enemies' canoes, and to cut off their retreat back again to the main, whilst our land party walked across the island, which was not more than a quarter of a mile broad, and commenced the attack.

I had not left Bonavidogo, but remained with him in his canoe, and just as we reached the other side and were right in among the enemies' small canoes, I heard the crash of murder on shore, some of the people being speared and clubbed just as they descended the coco-nut trees, and some as they were in the act of ascending or preparing to do so, and others as they were rushing along towards their canoes, which the one or two which had been left in each one were now fast paddling away, were either speared or shot down with muskets! But there was one man, who had rushed through the spears, clubs, tomahawks, handybillies, and musket balls of our murdering shore party unscathed, and into the water, towards the last of the small canoes, all the rest having got clear of the mêlée, paddling for their bare lives towards the main. This last and hitherto lingering small canoe was now being pulled away by one single paddle, following the rest, all of which were out of all danger now, and this poor fellow, who had already run such a terrible risk, was swimming after it in order to embark with his life. But Bonavidogo's large canoe was being sculled after him and fast coming up to him, but in the meantime some half a dozen muskets had been fired at him. He seemed to have a charmed life. Every shot had missed him.

Bonavidogo, although not the worst of this bad lot, in the excitement, something akin to the endeavouring to secure the last and escaping fish of a shoal, said to me, as I stood on the canoe's deck with my musket in my hand, "Why don't you fire and kill the 'Bakola?' "—in this sense a curse—"You can waste enough powder and lead at other times shooting worthless ducks!" By this time we were up with the swimming man, when Bonavidogo essayed to tomahawk him with his long-handled tomahawk from the canoe's decks which were not more than two feet above the water's surface, but I now interposed by placing myself betwixt him and his victim on the edge of the decks, the people still at the sculls, working to keep the canoe in position so that this man—who was more dead than alive with fright and exhaustion—could be despatched. I beseeched Bonavidogo not to kill him, but to turn him over to me. He struggled to accomplish his purpose. He did not attempt to strike me or to push me overboard—a thing he might perhaps have easily accomplished had he wished. Neither did the people interfere, pro or con. I had warded off the blows aimed at the head of the man several times, beseeching all the time, telling him to save him alive, so that we should be able to get the news of the movements of the general enemy the same as they do in "Vavalaga" (Europe), but all, at present, to no purpose. He said it was not

Fiji fashion ("Vaka Vite"). I told him that it was *humanity* fashion, asking him to place himself, in imagination, in that poor man's predicament. He was still obstinate, and so was I, and then I swore with exceedingly strong emphasis that he should not be killed whilst I was alive! Bonavidogo now desisted in a fashion, throwing his tomahawk on to the flat platform of the top of the canoe-house in disgust, saying, with an oath—an oath connected with one's mother!—that I could keep the *"Bakola,"* and see to it that he did not some of these nights show his gratitude by first murdering his benefactor, and then pilot the enemy on to themselves!

I now put out my hand to assist the poor fellow on board, but he was still afraid, when I told him to take a good look at my face, and see for himself that I was not like the rest of the canoe's crew, and that I was also more than master in the canoe. I got him on board at last, not without great difficulty, however, and then he clung to my legs with the most frantic terror, kneeling on the deck. I told him to try and re-collect himself and be at perfect ease regarding his life, but now the people seeing that he was really in a fair way of being saved, and which, up to the present, they did not believe to be possible—such a thing being, of course, entirely new to them—and as for the dispute I had had with the chief, they had looked upon that as a thing between father and son, and none of their business,—I say, that now that they saw that his salvation was a *bona fide* fact, they began murmuring among themselves, and then grunted audibly, and from that to clamouring for his life, when I jumped to an open space of the deck—there being plenty of room as the main portion of the crew were still on shore—cocked my musket and swore that I would shoot the first one who should offer to touch him. The prisoner, when I shifted my position, speedily followed me and was now crouching at my feet. I told these gentlemen, when they retorted that I would not be able to shoot but one—meaning, of course, that when the musket was discharged that they would be on top of me!—that I did not require the musket at all, that I would fight the whole of them, all at once with my dirk, laying the musket at my feet, defying them, and challenged them, one and all to come on, and that in a body and try it; and be speedy about it, or else I should in a very few seconds be among them! Of course I knew that all their muskets were discharged. I meant all I said whilst the passion lasted, and fully believed that I could cope with the whole of them together, picturing to myself what a pretty pastime it would be pulling the dirk out of one savage's heart and passing it into another's and so exterminate these ten or a dozen demons in human shape, whom I hated with an intensity not describable! They did not come to me, and, of course, I did not go to them, and so as I cooled down—after a storm always comes the calm—I held out to them the fact of their "Vasu Levu" having turned the prisoner over to me—a "Vasu Levu" means a person who is entitled to seize all kinds of property in the place which his mother is a native of, providing she is the daughter of a king or great chief, and that it was like their impertinence to attempt to thwart the decision of so high a personage!

The argument had the desired effect, and especially as Bonavidogo sat smiling as he was smoking his cigarette, highly amused, and even flattered by this speech of mine. The leading fellow of the clamourers went to the house of the canoe in midships and took a small white whale's tooth from his basket—articles they generally carry with them for cases of emergency when on the war-path, and especially when on the water—and presented it to me,

A SLIGHTLY REDUCED FAC-SIMILE OF A PAGE FROM THE
ORIGINAL MANUSCRIPT.

See page 34.

acknowledging aloud that he and his associates had behaved extremely wrong in opposing the decision of the "Vasu Levu," craving my pardon in the name of the gods of Neteva! I accepted the tooth and immediately handed it to the Neteva "Vasu."

This poor man's life was now effectually saved, and after a sufficient time had elapsed for him to be able to somewhat recover from his bewilderment, he answered the questions which Bonavidogo was now incessantly plying him with, quite to the satisfaction of that hero, regarding the intentions and movements of the "implacable enemy!"

Bonavidogo was now quite delighted that I had so effectually interfered for the salvation of this man's life and thanked me heartily, declaring that Fiji custom was all a lie, and that all Fijians, himself included, were fools, compared with Europeans! He then ordered a large dish of grog to be prepared, so that we could have a drink together, in order to re-cement the friendship which had hitherto existed between us, requesting his people, in a very mild and gentlemanly manner, that upon the recurrence of any of these disagreeable altercations, that they should immediately succumb to my better judgment, as he himself intended to do in future. We drank, each of us, our separate bowls of grog, simultaneously, whilst the people were chanting the short respectful imbibing song with the customary hand tattoo, which is performed by pretty sounding, lively, time-keeping claps, whilst anybody of note is in the act of imbibing.

During all this time we were proceeding in towards the shore by sculling—a process performed by sculls, somewhat resembling oars, being thrust through holes in the deck, left for that purpose, vertically, when each one is manned by a native as he stands in an upright position, and making a half-turn backwards and forwards, whilst he sways the upper part of his body in unison so as to augment the power required to propel the canoe along.

When we reached the shore the warriors (*alias* murderers) re-embarked, bringing the dead bodies ("bakolas") with them. They were set up in quite a formal array in two rows along the spacious decks, on their hind quarters, with their knees cocked up, and their hands lashed together over their knees so as to leave a space in the hind part of the bend of the same, to admit a long pole being rove through the bend of the same, each body supporting the other, as the whole row of bodies were in contact with each other. These gentlemen were quite *au fait* at this business, and no wonder, as they had all served their apprenticeships to the same, and had had plenty of practice ever since! Then they proceeded to cross-belt these quondam warriors with white tappa [1] crossed over their breasts, and their faces painted red, white or black, with a new head-dress over their heads of hair, exactly the same as though they were still alive and on the war-path—the object of all this was to deride them even after death—Fijians being extremely vindictive. In this way we arrived at Vida Point, when all the bodies were carried up the high hill—almost mountain—where the town of Naviu was situated, and duly presented to the God of War, "Dagei," at his temple, presided over by his priest, the young girls going through the usual degrading obscene rites with their antics over these much-abused bodies, and all for the sake of carrying revenge to the utmost extremity. They were then conveyed to the ovens and cooked, and then down the gullets of these determined cannibals!

[1] Native cloth made by beating bark.

CANNIBAL JACK

THAT night and the succeeding seven or eight, no native went to the house of his spouse, and indeed not till the purifying feast came off, however long that might be in abeyance—the usual prescribed period being ten nights.

They all slept in the different heathen temples. I happened to be in that dedicated to "Dagei" in the early part of the night, when a most extraordinary thing occurred to one of the natives who had accompanied us on the expedition. He was one who had always made himself very conspicuous on the war-path, and had long since succeeded to the much-coveted title of "Waga," and which title conveys its own meaning, i.e. that he had slaughtered enemies innumerable!

He was beside himself, and acted like a man who was possessed of as many devils as he had during his whole bloody career slaughtered enemies. He was lifting about, and sometimes with one hand only, things which no ordinary man in his right mind could by any possibility have moved, poising at one time a heavy log of wood in the shape of a spear, threatening to dart it end on in among us all, smashing old coco-nuts into atoms on his forehead, and reducing those very hard substances to fragments by the mere clutch of his right hand, just as though they were as fragile as hens' eggs! He was answering questions while his mouth was in a foaming state. The answers to these *supposed* questions were more than audible to the whole of the *then* inmates of the temple. These answers were in this wise: "I know your Majesty delights in blood!" "I'll kill more next time for your Majesty!" "Deal easy with me this time, *Saka!*"—equivalent to "your Majesty!" All these, answered in so emphatic and vehement a strain, conveyed the idea to the most obtuse and incredulous auditor—myself included—and especially as they were accompanied by the unheard-of feats of strength above mentioned, that "Dagei," the god of blood, war and rapine, was actually asking, and that angrily, the very questions which demanded and elicited these very answers! My poor prisoner's life at this critical time was far from safe; from the allusion that was made by the possessed in one of his answers to the name of "bobula bakola"—"dead! prisoner." And whether this farce—if farce it was?—was concocted by this crafty priest of this temple to extort whales' teeth, I knew not, neither did I care! but one thing I knew was essential to the preserving of my protégé's life, and that was a present to this arch-fiend of a priest, and I brought along three or four large yellow whales' teeth—yellow being more valued than white, even as much as gold is valued above silver among Europeans—and threw them in front of him; and although not given in the customary beseeching manner, they were too good to be refused by the avaricious son of the Fiji Church! He accepted them and immediately offered them to his master, "Dagei," with the usual prayer, and then the possessed recovered almost instantly. I told the Rev. J. Hunt of this circumstance, and which he quickly demolished, *à la missionary,* satisfactory to himself if not to me! He soon solved this most mysterious problem, by saying that God had not the slightest to do with the heathen Fijians, in consequence of the hardness of their hearts, and that he had long since turned them over to Satan, and that they were now really and truly his children and quite under his power, and that, in this case, as in all others, he was still urging them on to further evil, and that which I had witnessed was no farce at all, but the real power of the Devil!

CANNIBAL JACK

A LL this bustle and turmoil incident to these cannibal orgies, together with the multifarious
doing of the devil and a great many of his imps, had
scarcely subsided when the news came along up the
coast of "Vanua Levu" from the town of Monta,
situated up the mangrove creek before alluded to,
and where old Tue Macuaca resided, that that arch-
cannibal, ex-monarch, was on his death *mat*, and
that all and sundry of his relations, connexions, and
all adherents, and more especially his son Bonavidogo, should hurry up and hurry down before he
(his father) went down altogether—down to where?
God did not know and did not care, according to the
account of Mr. Hunt, the Superior of the Wesleyan
Society, but the Devil did, according to the account
of the same infallible authority; and so, in response
to this imperative message, we laid aside everything
pro tem., leaving the dead to bury the dead, and proceeded on down the coast, arrived at the mouth of
the creek, went up the same, passing all the nice
oysters, and at which my mouth greatly watered,
and with which I would much rather have lingered
than to have been in at the death of this old fox,
albeit he had killed a large hog for my individual
consumption, as soon as he learned, to his utter dis-

gust, that I preferred short pigs to long ones—long pigs being the facetious term for dead men! He had ordered this large hog to be dressed and cooked for me the last time I had been in his company. We arrived at the town at the head of the creek, where there were congregated quite a thousand darkies, he and she, and more almost every quarter of an hour still arriving. Among those from Macuaca was his eldest son by a Macuaca queen, consequently called "Vasu Taukei," and was entitled through his birth from this queen of the locality—his father being a native as well as king of the same place, although now expelled—to seize ("vasuka") any property not only from the rest of the Royal family and all its collateral branches, but from all the subjects residing in Macuaca, or any of its tributaries.

They were hammer and tongs howling and preparing to howl at the almost momently expected demise ("Ciba") of this arch-cannibal. All his wives were there ready, and willing too, apparently, to be strangled, in order to accompany him to those regions, where he would have to be waited upon in the same way as he had hitherto been in this, which he was now fast leaving. When I say they were *all* willing, there was one, at any rate, single exception, if I could judge by the forlorn expression and the wishful glance she was ever and anon casting at me! That one was the murdered Englishman's widow—the Rotama beauty. I made a very slight but expressive sign with my eyes that she was to retire from among the crowd and have an interview with me, and which she presently did without much difficulty. I watched her movements and soon after followed her. She told me that she wished me to run away with her before she was murdered. I immediately went to Bonavidogo, and although a most delicate question or subject on his part especially, I, without any preliminaries, entered upon it. I told him that she had not borne any children to his father, and that she was not a Fiji woman, and in her country the females never died at the death of their husbands, however much they loved them, and that, in reality, she ought to be turned over to me, seeing her former murdered husband was a fellow-countryman of mine, and that if he was as big and sagacious a chief as I had always given him credit for, he would concede to my prayer without any demur, and that immediately, as there was no time to be lost! He said that if it was in his power, *at all,* and not depending upon another, older and bigger than himself, inasmuch as that one was a "vasu" to the capital of the Macuaca kingdom, whereas he was himself but a vasu to a distinct and distant province, that he would forgo even the respect due to his father's remains for the sake of obliging me, but that I must consider that his half-brother was a distinct character entirely from himself by nature, owing perhaps to the character of his mother, who it was well known was a very austere woman compared with the lady who had given birth to himself. And likewise that the former was a great stickler for Fiji rites, and especially in this case, which so much concerned their father, and also that he was not, like himself, at all partial to whites, but the very opposite of that.

I left him, swearing that the woman should not die, and that I would test further, that very day, the friendship or otherwise, of himself towards me, even if it cost me my life! I went right away to where the woman had been waiting for my reappearance, and told her to come along whilst the breath was still in the body of her former husband's old murderer (her present husband had murdered her English husband and eaten him for the sake of herself). We left, not, however, exactly together, but I taking the lead, making a broad sheer clear of the concourse of this almost innumerable mob of negroes; she followed at a safe distance. As soon as we were quite clear we struck out with a will, leaving no grass growing beneath our feet. It came on dark, but we still continued our course in the direction of the place I had come from that morning in the canoe—i.e. up the coast towards Udu Point, hoping that we should eventually reach the town of Naviu, where I felt positive we should be safe, as it was under the jurisdiction of Bonavidogo, in whom I still had confidence, and what buoyed my hopes was, that I knew that the "Vasu Taukei's" influence did not even reach as far up the coast from Macuaca, which was a long way to leeward, as Monta—the town we had just left—itself, to say nothing of Naviu, which was a long way to windward. I knew also that he was not at all a popular character, and had only been tolerated in Monta at all on account of the shortly expected demise of his father. Udu Point was still a long way up the coast, but still I did not despair, but kept plodding along, urging the woman to further exertion, and to mend her pace, so as to increase our distance from Monta whilst dark, and then we could secrete ourselves in the bush to-morrow till the search was given up, and so killing

two birds with one stone as it were, she getting a rest
in the meantime, recruiting her strength, ready for
the renewal of the journey the next night.

WHILST I was buoying her up with hope all
the time, and my own spirits quite elated at
our anticipated success, all at once quite half a dozen
niggers were on top of us, from each side this track,
where they had been lying in ambush ahead of us!

They pounced upon us in an instant, disarmed me
of my musket, and took my cartridge box, sheath,
belt, and dirk, stripped us quite naked, and some of
them went further in the bush and procured a quantity of large green vines—as large as one's little
finger—whilst the others remained to keep guard
over us. With these vines, and which I distinctly remember—although now forty-five years ago—were
not very pliable but nearly as stiff as sticks, being so
large, they proceeded to lash us back to back, revers-
ing our heads—the one up, the other down—our
arms being strapped down by our sides with almost
innumerable turns with these stiff vines, and these
demons, in order to make them lie close, placed their
enormous big black hoofs against our persons as

though they had been logs of wood with no feeling (but what's the good of comparisons, when it's a well-known fact that these monsters do all these un-heard-of atrocities on purpose to torture, and these are some of the gentlemen which some missionaries crack up as saints, whereas even at the present day they are equally as bad as ever, if only an opportunity should crop up to show their hellish propensities! You can't wash the Ethiopian white!), sinking them more than half an inch thick into the more fleshy parts of our naked bodies, without, however, breaking our skins or causing blood to flow, but still stopping the natural circulation of the blood of the whole of our bodies. They then hung us up to the branch of a tree in a vertical position—the woman's head being upwards and mine downwards—and then decamped.

During the time they were doing all this I plied a number of questions, and the only answer I received was "makali," meaning, "not at all," "nothing of the kind," and although not appropriate answers—a thing they were totally regardless of—yet this word, or sentence rather, conveyed to me that they were Macuaca people, as there was no other dialect in all Fiji which had "makali" in it excepting the dialect of that place or its tributaries. It immediately occurred to me that this brutal piece of business had been instigated by the "Vasu Taukei," and I was greatly disturbed as to what the end of it might be; but I was soon relieved from all anxiety by my head seeming to be about the size of a bushel-basket and five or six times its weight, and then losing all consciousness! Lucky it was that the woman's head was in an upright position, and by that arrangement there seemed to be an object in view. That object was that she should not die but be reserved for a worse fate, previous to her final dissolution, and that fate was, that as she had absconded with me, she had shut herself from the alternative of meeting death by the more honourable (?) mode of being immolated to the manes of the old man-eater, and now that she could not by any means lay claim to virtue, and that the levity of her character was fully established in the minds of these obtuse brutes, they had concluded that she should have enough of it by turning her over to about a couple of hundred of these monsters, pending the decision of the Vasu Taukei, and to whom they had now gone to report progress and get further orders! As for me with my head downwards, if I died I would do to eat, and if found alive on their return they would revive me by feeding me on my own flesh, cooked or raw, according as their diabolical fancies struck them, and drinking my own blood!

But *"L'homme propose et Dieu dispose!"* for, all at once, consciousness began to dawn upon me, and yet I could not tell where I was, or what was being done to me, or by whom. I saw the woman by my side sitting up. There was also a third person squeezing my flesh with both his hands over the indents of the vines, which were now clear of our bodies. This manipulation I soon perceived was intended to restore circulation. I also perceived by whom it was being done. It was my poor prisoner whom I had saved from Bonavidogo's tomahawk. After a while he lifted us both to our feet, and although very stiff we managed to walk by the assistance of this faithful fellow, one on each side of him; and when the track became so narrow and bad, we still managed to follow him slowly, in Indian file, one behind the other, and lucky for us that we had not far to go. We made the head of a deep-water creek where there was a small canoe with a paddle in it and a piece of bamboo for bailer. There was also a pole stuck through the interstices of the lattice-work of the outrigger, down into the mud to keep it from drifting away. We all three embarked, when he pulled up the pole and paddled away towards the mouth of the creek, and which we soon reached. And now he took the pole and poled along up shore towards Udu Point. He proceeded along in this way for upwards of an hour, without speaking a single word, making the canoe almost fly, stopping every ten or fifteen minutes to rapidly scoop out the water with the piece of bamboo and throw it over the side, renewing the poling again. At last, when Udu Point was in sight and nothing could be seen behind us that we need be afraid of, he slackened up and poled along more at his leisure, he being considerably winded by the over-exertion he had undergone. I bailed now that I was getting better, although the marks of the vines did not entirely leave either of our bodies for nearly a month. As soon as we had rounded the last point excepting the one of "Udu," he burst out laughing, exclaiming aloud, "Sa bula," equivalent, in this case, to safely escaped!

I now perceived, as the daylight was breaking, that he had got my sheath knife buckled around him with its belt. I asked him where he had fallen in with it? He said that he had picked it up from under the branch of the tree from which he had lowered us, the Macuaca "baolas" having dropped it again in their hurry to get back again to the Vasu Taukei for further orders regarding us. He said that when I was leaving Bonavidogo, and had so incautiously and in such a loud tone sworn that the woman should not die, and whilst in that violent passion, he had heard me, and the Vasu Taukei had heard me too, and then he immediately went to Bonavidogo and apprised him that his white man was in danger, when he told him to leave his presence at once and scout about slyly, and, apparently, unconcerned, and learn all he could, and rescue me and the woman too by the best means he could devise, reminding him that his own life depended upon my safety, because if I was killed, he being my "bobula" he would become a lawful prey to anyone who thought proper to kill him, and besides, my own friends would clamour for his death as well as the death of all my wives as sacrifices to my manes!

He then started off on his errand, and seeing some commotion in the Vasu Taukei's quarters, he there learned that he was despatching off different parties on the two or three different roads, very quietly, to cut us off, or overtake us; and as he himself thought

it more than likely that I would try to make back to
Naviu, he had followed that party at a distance behind, unperceived by them, and that they had followed the branch track, which made a sweep further
into the bush, leading into a village which was now
deserted, but still leading up the coast the same as
the one I had followed, the only difference being
that my road was nearer the salt water and lay to the
left, whereas theirs trended obliquely to the right,
and after getting through the village it wound round
again and became one track with the one I had followed; but as they had followed on with all speed,
having no female with them as in my case, of course
they had got ahead of us, hence our capture. He
said the moment they had left us two hanging to
the branch, and that he heard the pattering of their
retreating feet, he was himself up the tree, and as
the vine was long with which they had suspended us,
he lowered us gently down, but had the end of the
vine been cut short, and he had cut us down, we
should have been inevitably killed, and I especially
should have my neck broken, seeing my head was
downwards. The reason the end of the vine was
left long and uncut was that they had not taken the
knife up the tree, and which they had lost and es-

sayed to find, but being dark they had given it up. He also told me that had the end of the vine been cut, and he thereby been necessitated to bend on the same or look for another, the delay would have proved fatal by me being suffocated, and that I was some good little time coming to myself as it was, and that he was lucky in picking up the knife with which he severed the ligatures, but had he had no knife, he should have been obliged to roll our bodies over and over in order to get those very many turns off with speed, and, no doubt, it would have proved fatal, to me, at any rate!

It appears the latter part of the threat which I had used when I last left Bonavidogo proved almost prophetic in two ways, i.e. that I almost lost my life as well as tested his friendship for me, and found it genuine in spite of all drawbacks. And so to the gratitude of my prisoner, or rather protégé, I have no occasion to complain, notwithstanding what has been said, and written too, about the "ingratitude" of Fijians, but then they never experienced Fijians as I have, and especially in the early period of Fijian history.

CANNIBAL JACK

WE arrived safe and sound—a little stiffness excepted—at the town of Naviu, where we were quickly supplied with clothing, I with the native tappa or "masi" and my newly acquired and hard-worked-for wife, with a quantity of "likus," [1] brought in from different houses by the hospitable inmates. They also quickly concocted different savoury messes and brought along to the house where my other three wives were staying whilst on their visit to Naviu until the time came round for our return to Neteva. These three ladies received this new accession to the harem with open arms and hearts too, declaring that she should be their "marama" (queen). My protégé related the whole adventure, dilating considerably on the whole occurrence, and which I did not in the least try to check. He also told the Naviu people that I was not wholly reconciled as to our safety in regard to the Vasu Taukei, whom they, one and all with the greatest indignity, declared that they did not acknowledge him in the least, and that they only knew his brother Bonavidogo through his mother being a great "marama" (lady) of Neteva, and his own good character as well as his warlike propensities which were a

[1] Skirts.

36

great advantage to them in defending them from the common enemy, and that Naviu was his particular pet town, although he had "dua tale na drau in koro"—a hundred others!

In a few days afterwards the Neteva fleet of canoes arrived with all the warriors of that place, and Bonavidogo at their head, from Monta, having buried the cannibal-king with all his wives, besides all the things he had used in life in the shape of whales' teeth, etc., etc., not omitting the skull of one of the hundreds of "baolas" he had devoured during his cannibal existence, and which he had used for years as his "yogona" drinking-bowl. This particular skull had been selected for that purpose on account of the extraordinary difficulty his people had in defeating this leading king-warrior, and after years of contest the downfall was achieved of this implacable enemy! And so every time he imbibed his faith was renewed that "nothing was impossible to him!" The skewer-like fork constructed from the leg bone of this tough old warrior, and with which Tue Macuaca used to eat his human flesh from, was also interred with him.

The Vasu Taukei, when he found that I had slipped his fingers—consequently his gullet—by some means or other, and what they were he never learned, sent the musket to Bonavidogo which his people had taken from me, and which of right belonged to the latter. He also sent a whale's tooth, apologizing for his people interfering with his white man, unknown to himself, he said! And so, all's well that ends well!

AFTER the Naviu people had made a feast for Bonavidogo, condoling with him for the great bereavement he had sustained by the loss of his father, Tue Macuaca, and we had all partaken of it together, and that there was nothing more of consequence to be done here, and especially as Naviu had been considerably drained of food, having been laid under quite a contribution for some time past by the Neteva warriors, as well as all the camp followers, composed of women, heathen priests, girls, wives, wives' sisters, and some of their mothers, servants of both sexes, old men, old women, loafers, "*et hoc omnus geni,*" and lastly, if not leastly, white man— myself, we put all the riches composed of Fiji property, mostly, with a small sprinkling of European, or rather American goods, composed of a musket or

CANNIBAL JACK

two, one or two rifles, some pistols, double-barrelled shot guns, powder flasks, shot belts, cartridge boxes, bayonets, cutlasses, axes, tomahawks, knives, and some bushels of the inevitable whales' teeth, besides some dozen or so blankets—white, red and blue; pieces of print calico, etc.—the source of all these things being the American bêche-de-mer,[1] from the port of Salem in the State of Massachusetts, U.S.A. There were also lots of flints, percussion gun caps, ball moulds, etc., etc.; the most of these things had been acquired by Bonavidogo "koving" (seizing) from all the places we visited up and down the coast, and all on the strength of his being the son of the "marama levu" (great lady) of Neteva! I say, we put all these things on board our fleet and embarked ourselves. A portion of all his property had been given by relations through intermarriages—this latter being performed by betrothment in infancy, irrespective of the principals in the contract giving their sanction—indeed, they have no choice in the matter, either at the time when entered into, being hardly possible on account of their tender ages—or at the time when arrived at the stage of puberty, because in the latter term it would be too late to recall, as

[1] Bêche-de-mer: a sea slug, much prized as food by the Chinese.

presents innumerable had been received, mostly from the parents of the male, given to the parents of the female. I say, after all the riches had been safely stowed on board the canoe, we embarked ourselves— I and my four concubines as well as my faithful "bobula" to whom I now owed my life, as he had previously owed his to me, and so, as the obligation was now reciprocal, no wonder that the attachment was the same, and if we two could not trust each other, I don't know who could! And now came the parting, a thing, when the visit has been prolonged to an indefinite period, of the utmost difficulty, with this, in some cases, really sensitive people.

Strange to say, that although they, in hatred, go to the utmost verge of insanity, itself, by actually absorbing their enemies into the third or lower stomach itself, yet, on the other hand, in friendship, they being possessed of such an abnormal share of sentiment, that they become knit with a perfectly indissoluble reciprocity; and so, at this parting, as with all others, under similar circumstances, it was really affecting and heartrending to witness, as I did, the bewailing accents, accompanied with copious floods of genuine tears, and the clinging with the last and most ardent embraces of these, in many respects, most wonderful people—to make a long story short, they never do anything by halves! The girl-visitors get attached to the young fellows of the place to such a degree that they have frequently to be torn away at their parting embrace by sheer violence, notwithstanding that this scene is being witnessed, in some cases, by some hundreds of spectators, of both sexes, in broad daylight, their betrothed being among them! The very same thing, not infrequently, happens even with the married women, their husbands witnessing it much to their discomfort; and yet very seldom does anything bad or immoral come out of it—it being sentimental, not carnal! In these latter cases the husband generally acts, to all appearance, quite philosophically, however different he may feel! He tries to console himself by taking the whole blame upon himself for taking her with him at all, and especially, on these long expeditions, but then he acted for the best, seeing there was quite as much danger incurred by leaving her at home! And then his love-lorn spouse, after a pining melancholy mood for nearly or quite a month, will come round of her own accord—being cured by the panacea—time! And now he has a lesson which will last him, if not for life, as long as will be requisite,

CANNIBAL JACK

i.e. till the "yellow and sere" begins to set in, on his wife, and then he can take or leave her at home with impunity!

After having my musketry tools—consisting of a hammer, pincers, one or two files, screw-driver, together with some old leather, salt, bone, etc., for putting fire into the hammers of flintlock muskets, besides a bag full of scissors, mainsprings, feathersprings, hammer-springs, dogs, tumblers, plates, etc., etc.,—in fact, every conceivable portion of the locks of old muskets, which I had scraped together from time to time, during my frequent tours in pursuit of my business—musket mending,—and affording me thereby every facility of acquiring the much-coveted tortoiseshell, I say, after having all these things brought on board, besides all the tortoiseshell I had accumulated on this trip, by my "man Friday," we set sail, and that afternoon arrived safe and sound at my home, Neteva, situated about half-way down on the port side of "Wai tue mate" (dead salt water) in this very deep bay, or more properly firth or estuary.

CANNIBAL JACK

A FTER a day or so of our arrival, these moon-
stricken damsels, to make matters worse with
their affianced or betrothed lovers, and husbands
even, congregated together, condoling with each
other on the loss of their affections during their late
escapade, and actually docked off the two joints of
the left-hand little finger of every one of them! in
commemoration of the great grief they had
sustained in the loss of their hearts in their late romantic attachments—a rite universally acknowleged
and performed throughout the whole group on the
exit by decease of their relatives, or even when any
calamity befalls them short of death, and called in
Fiji ("loloku"), mourning, I suppose. And in fact,
throughout the various islands and groups of the
whole of the North and South Pacific Ocean, notwithstanding their different breeds and origin, and
being distinct peoples, physically and religiously, and
yet this or some other mode of hacking or maiming
is observed at the death of a chief or relative; as,
for instance, when some years after this event, when
I resided on the west coast of the largish island of
New Caledonia and kept a harem—or rather perhaps they kept me—they kept me busy at any rate—
of some thirty females as concubines or wives,

whichever is the most proper term, one of them at the death of her father, Bume, the king of Koni, during the performance of this very drastic self-inflicted rite, actually beat her brains out with two stones, one in each hand, and of course, died! Her life was curtailed, in the first place, for a lack of quantity of that very essential natural ingredient, and then, for the want of it altogether, of course, she found that more befitting state which she was naturally adapted to—death! as, of course, she had no business to live, or, in fact, anyone else who cannot estimate life at its proper value! And then again, as another example, of the many thousands I could cite, were it necessary, the Usu or Wallis Island people—a race of the yellow-skinned and straight-haired "kanaka" [1] or Malay type, on the death of one of their subordinate chiefs; and during the performance of one of the prettiest war-dances I ever witnessed by these very handsome people, I saw, what most people would term a most shocking scene of wholesale wounding, deliberately perpetrated in order to extract blood—the universal desideratum for showing the grief or sorrow which is being undergone for the loss sustained, as well as

[1] Kanaka: a South Sea islander; equivalent to our term Nigger.

for the propitiation required upon all such occasions!
It happened thus:—Two rows of natives, all males
—about sixty in each row—stood opposite each
other, some single men, some married, about four or
five feet apart, each row facing the other, one row
armed with bayonets on the end of carved wooden
handles about five feet long, for the purpose of
offence or defence, as the case might be—the other
row armed with clubs, spears, and tomahawks, and
after going through various very expert pretty
antics, in the shape of making blows, darting spears,
and thrusting with the bayonets, and fending and
warding off with the same for some considerable
space of time, to the great amusement and acclama-
tions of the bystanders—male and female—all at
once, by a preconcerted arrangement, it being part
and parcel of the performance, the whole of the men
composing the bayonet row, as they danced in con-
cert on one of their legs, suspending the other some
little distance from the ground, the knee being bent,
and whilst they held these sharp implements firmly
by the handles with both hands, thrust the whole
length of the bayonet completely through their
suspended thighs, and then reversed the order of the
dance, by dancing on the wounded legs and then

served the hitherto unwounded legs in the very same way—so that one leg could not laugh at the other, a waggish native bystander told me! They then went on with the dance as though nothing extra had happened, till human nature had to succumb, when they fell wallowing in pools of their own blood, when some were led away, and more had to be carried off to their houses!

As I had now on hand a good little quantity, over a ton, of tortoiseshell, and as one of the schooner tenders for the bêche-de-mering brig was constantly running round in search of that commodity, as well as collecting the sea-slug from the different stations, I made up my mind all in a moment, as it were, that I would proceed on to Manilla, and especially as the brig had now completed her cargo, with my shell. I sold a quantity to this tender for a few firearms and ammunition and gave the same to Bonavidogo, and then took passage myself for Macuaca with the rest of it—the brig lying at this latter place. I secured a passage for myself and shell from the captain by payment of dollars which I

46

had first received from himself for a portion of the shell.

I had left my four wives in charge of Bona-vidogo, the chief, a Neteva, with strict injunctions as to their usage during my absence, which might be a year—it might be two—I told him, but if I did not return at the expiration of these years, to let the women take their choice of husbands, and upon no account to imagine I was dead, but conclude that I had gone to England, and that I had given up Fiji for ever. I also left strict orders with my "bobula" —leaving him all my arms—to attend constantly to the women till my return. I also left a quantity of Yankee knick-knacks—useful as well as ornamental —for my wives, an extra quantity for the Rotama lady, as she ruled the whole household. Immediately after this, the brig had on board her usual quantity of bêche-de-mer, from 1,500 to 2,000 pikul of this valuable commodity—worth, the No. 1 quality, called in Fiji "sucu walu" (eight teat fish) and another species of the same genus, called black fish, being of the same colour as the former, quite $100 the "pikul," a weight of lbs. 133½—making the whole cargo worth the great sum of $12,500 or £2,500 in English money.

CANNIBAL JACK

We met with nothing worthy of note to make a book out of, as we had generally a leading, if not exactly a fair wind, during this passage. But, I may as well mention in this place, the very ingenious as well as dangerous modes the "kanakas" of some of the islands we passed have of capturing the sea monsters—sharks. Boys from fourteen to sixteen years old, generally, go in twos and threes. If a single large shark was seen from their canoe, one of these boys would immediately lower himself into the water with his baited two-barbed piece of hard wood, sticking out at right angles from the main stem of this tough stick of about four feet in length, and ply it towards the shark's nose, and Johney shark, nothing loth, would almost directly close his jaws and so pin them together, if not exactly permanently, long enough for the second boy to get under him with his sharp butcher's knife, and rip away at his throat or belly; whilst the third boy would have hold of his tail, and then jump on his back and pommel away at this monster's hard head as if for bare life, with his short bludgeon, and by these concerted means these smart and brave lads would in a very short time render this brute *hors de combat!*

CANNIBAL JACK

Grown men would sometimes encounter a large shark with the butcher's knife, alone, single-handed, and capture him too! The China merchants, after we had arrived safe and sound in Manilla, met us there and purchased all the cargo, and the captain then laid in a quantity of goods, in the shape of vermilion, beads, etc., etc., requisite for the Fiji trade, and then returned again to that cannibal country in order to secure a second cargo for Manilla, and after that on to the United States of America, taking, in all, from three to three and a half years—and two voyages like this occupying from six to seven years, would, if all went well, secure to himself a competency for the rest of his life; and so this being the case with the captain, even, I leave it to the sagacious reader to compute what enormous profits must accrue to the owner in this most lucrative trade. The captain inquired of me if I wished to return to my adopted home of Fiji with him, as he should be most happy of my company. I told him, No, not at present, and so I remained behind with my upwards of a thousand pounds which I had received for my shell—this Manilla being about as good a market as any in the world, I suppose, for a limited quantity of that article, in consequence of high black combs for the fair sex being all the rage—the four big, main, back pieces, from the back of this amphibious animal, fetching an enormous price for that purpose, the rest and inferior portions generally reaching China, where they were used principally for veneering, fancy toys, furniture, etc., etc., and consequently realized but an inferior price. I had a look at most of the amusements and pastimes of this large Spanish colonial capital, which consisted of bull baits, cock fighting, dancing dogs, fandangos—by the ladies principally, in the various "poolpoises" or public houses, or drinking saloons, but as most of these things have been described time and again, by various and abler narrators, as well as the whole of the Philippine Islands, and more especially as it is a place of great trade, producing hemp, rope, bees' wax, sugar, etc., etc., and some two or more centuries old, it does not come under my plan—my narrative being almost entirely confined to newer island life, consequently less known.

I soon had enough of all this, albeit occasionally varied by the sight of a hand-to-hand duel-like encounter of the Spanish-bred mongrel Indians with their "kajilas" (knives) in the not infrequent brawls

CANNIBAL JACK

kicked up in the low shanties of the back slums of
this large motley-populated place, when they would
be conveyed off by the "quaterjecos," and if one
should chance to die of his wounds, the other, if he
escaped being shot, although perhaps not aggressive,
would be accommodated with government rations,
consisting of corn maize, and which he would have
to grind himself, together with plenty of work,
whilst he dragged about a large heavy ball, attached
to the end of a longish chain, the other end being
securely fast to his ankle, for the next ten years, at
least, of his very pleasant life—perhaps twenty, perhaps for the rest of his *"natural life"* ! "Desperate
diseases require desperate remedies," as the "Gov-
ernador" so well knew, and acted upon, during the
occurrence of the insurrection which happened in
this place, years after my visit, when he called out
the troops to quell this large rising, notwithstanding
the presence of the numerous Catholic priests or
"padres" dressed in their rosaries, crucifixes, and
all the rest of the popish paraphernalia incident to
the regalia of Holy Mother Church, interceding with
due pomp and ceremony on their bended knees, perhaps, backed up with the names of a great many
saints of the Romish calendar, besides the queen of

51

heaven, for their lives only, when he, with more decision than mercy, told them to pray for their souls, and give absolution in a kind of job lot, for there was no time to be lost, seeing that their bodies were forfeited, commanding the troops to fire, and which they promptly did, stretching their lifeless corpses to the number of 150 on the ground, and so quelled this abnormal uprising with one blow, as it were! And if this more than seemingly severe measure cannot but be condemned, yet the decision, if it cannot exactly be applauded, must be somewhat admired, inasmuch as it saved the place and prevented, more than likely, greater horrors! which these most horrible semi-barbarians—and especially since their mixture with the hot-blooded Spaniards from Europe—are quite capable of perpetrating! This people, if not kept in subjection, is perhaps, by nature one of the worst races under the sun!

I NOW took passage to different ports of China and India—in fact, went from one to the other in search of that which I did not find—content—neither did I find its equivalent—amusement. It was neither savage nor civilized! But, after seeing their cities, rivers, sampans, josses, junks, pig-tails, eating rice with chopsticks, conjuring, serpent charming, juggling, ships with eyes to see where to go to when their masters did not know; jungles, tigers, and the hunting of them:—nabobs, indigo growers, pagodas and even Juggernaut itself, nautch girls, and the nautch dancing, eating their "dholl" and "ghee" and riding on their elephants and in their sedans and kept warm by their curries and cool by their punkahs, and for all of which it cost me £600, when I paid my passage back to Manilla and then to Fiji.

As we neared Fiji, the wind being somewhat un-favourable, the first land we made was "Fortuna" or Horne Islands, one of the Friendly Islands, not more than twenty-four hours' sail from Fiji (i.e. with a fair wind); but as we were close in, and as I had been there before, and which the cap-tain had learned by my conversation, he asked me if I would oblige him by going on shore in a boat and purchase for him a boatload of fresh provisions, when I told him I would, and that I should stay there for a time, seeing that I could get to Fiji at almost any time, I thought, it being so handy. I, accordingly, after purchasing a barrel of flour, a quantity of salt-beef and pork, a bag of sugar, some tea and coffee, a bag of spice, a piece of calico and ditto of print, besides some knick-knacks—commonly called "small trade," and some powder and flints, percussion caps, and also a couple of demijohns of the China spirituous liquor called (in China) "samshu." After putting all these things in the boat and bidding adieu to the captain and officers, crew, cook and steward, I proceeded to the shore. Here I saw Sam the king, my former shipmate, some five years previous, and although he did not know me, I having so altered by the rough usage of the world, and more so by the rougher usage I had given myself, yet I knew him instantly, and when I made myself known to him, the delight was reciprocal, he being a "kanaka" of course there was not the slightest doubt about the feeling on his part, as there might have been had he belonged to what is generally termed the "superior race," there being too much conventionality generally in the latter, and so it is somewhat difficult to distinguish between it and genuineness!

The boat was filled in about half an hour, the natives having rushed off to their gardens the moment they saw the boat leaving the ship's side—with pigs, turtle, ducks, turkeys, fowls, and vegetables of every description, which are indigenous to the tropics, besides a multiplicity of various descriptions of fruit which happened to be in season. The boat pushed off and stood for the ship, and then all my things were immediately conveyed up to Sam's large white-washed house by the people, when he immediately gave me two large rooms and a kitchen adjoining.

There were on the island, at this time, three young white men, sailors who had some few weeks previous absconded and taken to the bush when the boats of an American whaler, to which they had belonged, came on shore for the sake of replenishing their stock of fresh provisions—this island being particularly prolific in such things—and so had effectually, for the time being at any rate, evaded their capture by the natives, which these latter were exceedingly desirous of accomplishing for the sake of the pretty heavy reward which is generally offered in these cases, and now that they had slipped their fingers, and their ship had proceeded on her cruise in search of whales, the natives looked upon these somewhat forlorn youths with anything but favour or pity! The same old story! This ship had been commanded by one of those Yankee tyrants, which was at that time so very prevalent in the whaling trade! These poor fellows had for clothing only what they stood in, and these were all in tatters. I supplied them with a quantity of strong unbleached calico sufficient to make each of them a couple of "jumpers" and trousers, quite adapted to the torrid zone, and as I wanted company and had plenty of room, besides I wished to show the somewhat avaricious kanakas a good example, and lastly, and principally, if I may state the real fact of the case, my heart yearned over them, consequently I invited them to stay with me altogether and take pot-luck.

We amused ourselves by showing the native girls how to cook, and concocted really good and savoury messes. We had baked sucking pigs, which I could purchase for a yard of common print, or a ten cent butcher's knife, or perhaps even for a couple of large fish-hooks. We had our tea regularly, using as milk the cream-like liquid from the meats of the old coconuts, flour mixed with ripe bananas and then fried with hog's head made very tasty pancakes, *alias* "flapjacks." The "samshu" we used with hot water, sugar, limes, lemons, or citrons—whichever came first to hand—there was also ginger and other things innumerable in the shape of spices, etc., and which the natives made no use of because they considered them worthless. There were also myriads of oranges. Whenever eggs were found they were always brought to me to sell for some trifle such as a piece of tobacco or a small fish-hook, and as I was the only market on the island, of course I always had them, not only in dozens, but sometimes in hundreds!

We varied the intoxicating beverage by making a copious use of the juice of the root here called "kava" and which is exactly the same as the Fiji "yagona."

The girls were kind, affable, courteous, pleasant, and quite taken up with these young fellows, and these in their turn became quite spoony on some of them, but then they were Roman Catholics, and if a foreigner wanted a wife, he had to become a "good Catholic" instead of a "heretic" as the two French priests had taught them to so designate all strangers! This "good Catholic" business would, of course, be subject to the priests' approval as to its genuineness. Besides all this, these poor chaps lived in daily and hourly jeopardy lest their ship should return again, and then by the offer of the much coveted rewards, the natives would be sure to pounce upon them and deliver them up to the captain, who would be sure to augment his tyrannical cruelty for the rest of the voyage if he once again ever got them into his clutches!

The tyranny they might expect, if captured, would be in the first place, a sound, unmerciful, severe flagellation, laid on with a will, in order to enable the "Old Man to see the backbone of these tarnation skunks," extra mastheads, no watch below for the rest of the voyage, even if it lasted a year or two, but get sleep as they could catch it by stealth, subject to a bucket of cold salt water thrown over them by the officers—who are always of one mind with the "Old Man" in these things—night or day, in whatever latitude the ship happened to be in. And touched up occasionally, just merely to freshen the nip, with the lash, just as the maggot bites, in order to relieve the "Old Man's" spleen, and especially when no whales had been seen from the mastheads for some time past!

CANNIBAL JACK

THESE French "pères," *alias* Jesuits, or their successors, they might have been, seeing that it is not much over a dozen years since it happened, it being '75 or '76 of our Lord, met with a mistake when they interfered—at least, one of them did, because, I believe, in this last-mentioned date, there was but one concerned, perhaps the only one on the island at the time—I say he met with a mistake when he interfered with Proctor, a one-legged American trader, and, by the by, one of those wonderfully brave men which are so often met with in the Pacific. It happened thus:—Proctor had taken to himself a female partner, without the consent of the "père," not thinking it necessary, as she was a half-caste daughter of a former trader—a European Portuguese, by, I believe, a Samoan mother, and so, if so, both father and mother foreign to the island, in consequence of which fact, the priest had no earthly control whatever over her, neither had he over Proctor, but yet he must be meddlemaking according to their craft, and so he went to their house to drag the woman away by force. He was accompanied by his kanaka-myrmidons, and after insisting in the most imperious language, which most of these people know so well how to assume

59

CANNIBAL JACK

upon all such occasions! Proctor objected, giving all the reasons, and dared them to enter his home, but still all to no effect. They rushed in, headed by the priest, and, by his orders, laid violent hands on the woman. Proctor being, for years past, a pistol-man, had recourse upon this occasion, as well as upon many former ones, to the seldom-failing convincing argument, by placing the muzzle of his little bulldog within an inch of this overbearing son of the Church's ear, and swore that he would blow his brains out if they did not desist, and as they did not, he, of course, being a man of his word, proceeded to do so by pulling the trigger, but the cap only snapped and the pistol did not go off, lucky for the bead-counter, or else he would have found himself in that place which they *think* they are bound to quicker than all the saints, not excluding the adorable Mary, could have escorted him to! Proctor was now handled in a very rough manner by the myrmidons, who were ordered by this exemplary and merciful leader, instead of turning the other ear as recommended by the great prototype of all forbearance!

A French man-of-war called here in a few days after this occurrence, and as the captain had more sense than the Jesuit, he merely gave Proctor a passage to Levuka in Fiji, whither the ship was bound, and left him there. An American man-of-war soon after this, saw into this affair, and awarded Proctor some great sum to be paid by Fortuna in copra or coco-nut oil, and not to exceed two years in completing the last instalment of the fine to be received as damages by Proctor; but I never heard any more of the matter, and I believe that was the last of it. Uncle Sam is generally very prodigal of his awards, ten, fifteen, and even twenty thousand dollars, and sometimes out of all proportion to the injury sustained; but then, by some means or other, it is hardly ever forthcoming, as in the case of poor old George Rodney Birt, when the Viti Levu cannibals, up the Sigatoka River, some seventeen years ago, upset his large cotton-plantation, killing and eating his horses, pigs and half-caste child, besides ravishing its mother by some scores—perhaps hundreds—of these demons in human shape, feeding his Tuna labour on their own flesh, besides many other atrocities too revolting to enumerate! I don't know the exact amount awarded in this case, but something between 20,000 and 50,000 dollars! But, as I said above, the award and nothing more. Nothing but wind with Yankees!

But then John Bull is much worse. He seldom awards at all, and hardly ever inquires, and if he does, it is generally settled against the poor unfortunate white, who perhaps has barely succeeded in getting clear by the skin of his teeth with his bare life, after fighting against one hundred odds, and extricated himself by the most unheard-of exploits of bravery, and then Mr. Bull awards him, perhaps, with ten years' penal servitude, and the only wonder is that he was not hanged!

The Germans and French located in these seas are the best Governments for their subjects to seek redress from for injuries sustained at the hands of the savages, either by fine, when practicable, or by pitching straight into them by fire and sword, seldom lacking the will to perform these much required punishments, but sometimes fail through the crafty alacrity of the black rascals in keeping out of the way!

A ND now, after this somewhat, of what the impatient reader by a stretch of imagination might term a longish digression, I will resume the

main topic of my narrative, for the delectation of
this said supposed reader, by reverting again to
these greenhorns, my house-mates, the Yankee *sea-
men* who were enjoying themselves on the best of
everything the islands produced, besides many of
the productions of half the world as well: to wit—
print and calico from England, for clothing; America for the flour, beef and pork; China for the rice
and samshu, tea, etc.; and Manilla for the sugar,
and instead of retiring every day to the top of a
hill or mountain as I should have done—or they
might have spared one hand to keep a constant look
out, and made it by turn and turn about, knowing
the risk they ran by remaining constantly in the
house, and especially as they were aware that that
part of the ocean was quite a good whaling ground,
and, in fact, all around for hundreds of miles, I having myself, before and since, assisted to capture some
of the largest sperm whales in the vicinity of Wallis'
Island, Rotuma, Tongatabu, etc., etc., and more
than likely their "Old Man" would give another call
for the sake of capturing this part of his missing
crew.

They were continually fretting about a wife each
—a thing that would not have entered their heads

in their own country, and yet they were always bemoaning their hard fate lest they should be recaptured! At last I told them that I could prevent the latter calamity befalling them and give them a wife each besides, if they would only go with me to Fiji. They asked where the vessel was. I told them we would lash two small canoes together. They then asked how far it was. I told them that it was about 200 miles to the part I wished to go to, in order to be safe, as the islands of Fiji could not be rushed upon with impunity, because most of them were inhabited by the most determined cannibals, and were not only addicted to killing people, but would, in all cases, after that little business was consummated, eat them, besides, even if they were their own brothers, because their very religion taught them to do so; but, as a set-off to this most horrible account, they would be all right in my company if all went as I anticipated. They agreed to go, saying that, as I was an Englishman, they believed all I said, and that it was certain that I must myself believe in the practicability of this run to Fiji, or else I should not be so foolish as to venture it; and besides I was the oldest, and had had experience in these kind of things. And, besides, if I was not afraid, "why should they be?" they said.

We accordingly had an extra cup or two of the "samshu" to confirm this agreement, and the next morning I purchased a couple of smallish single canoes, with perfectly sound bodies, took off their outriggers, but left the lattice-work stretching from the tops of each canoe, and to which the outriggers had been suspended, and then telescoped, as it were, this lattice-work one into the other and so doubled it, lashed them solidly together, leaving the canoes about four feet apart, and formed a deck by lashing pieces of strong saplings fore and aft, making all exceedingly firm and strong. We then got two shortish sapling-masts, made two sails from unbleached calico, took vines for rigging, a large stone for an anchor, another vine for a cable, filled our empty demijohn with fresh water, diluted the half demijohn of samshu which was left, added lime juice and sugar and so filled it up, it being now what men-of-war's men term "one-watered grog," and exactly the thing. We now baked three or four large dampers without leaven, cooked three or four pieces of pork and beef, got four or five poles for poling along in shoal water when we reached Fiji, four or five paddles besides sculls, which latter answered well for oars, put my chest in midships between the two masts, and lashed it firm, left tobacco, pipes, and matches on the top of everything so as to be got at, at any moment, for a chew or a smoke, got two or three large roots of "kava" from Sam, the king, as presents to the Fiji chiefs at our introduction, and then, almost the last thing, had about 150 green coco-nuts thrown from the trees and stowed away in the holes of the canoes, out of the way of where we intended bailing if water should come in, left the most of the goods and provisions for Sam's use, bid him good-bye, and started, one fine afternoon, at about five o'clock, the wind being about east.

We kept her as close to the wind, at first starting, as she would lie, so as not to stop her way by shaking, in order to keep well to the windward of the Macuaca coast of Vanua Levu, lest we might get potted; but the next morning I kept her off two points so as to rattle her over the water, lest by dilly-dallying we might be overtaken by bad weather.

We kept her going in this manner all the next night, till about eleven o'clock the next day, when we saw land and made for it. We now down on our bended knees and offered a heartfelt prayer and thanksgiving to the Almighty Providence which had guided us safely so far in that frail canoe without any mishap, and beseeching His still protecting care for the rest of the run to our destination. After this we sat up quite refreshed but rather hungry. We then had a good feed of damper, beef and pork and washed all down with the young coco-nuts, the milk of which we got at by cutting off the ends of some dozen of these goblets, which were as fresh as ever, and washed all down by about half a pint of the diluted samshu each. I now proceeded to load our four muskets with a cartridge each, which we had made before we started. These muskets I had purchased on quite easy terms from the Fortuna natives, as there was now no need of firearms since they had embraced the Catholic religion at the hands of the French priests.

W E were making fast up to the island all this time, and about two o'clock, I suppose it must have been by the appearance of the sun, the only watch or even compass we had for this precarious kind of navigation, excepting the stars, by night, and as one constellation or single star dipped below the horizon, so we took another higher up, each night, till the daylight broke in the eastward. The wind and the heave of the sea were quite a helpful guide in our calculations. At about two o'clock we were on the lee side of the island and the water was quite smooth, and lucky it was for us that our vessel was so slight a draught of water —only a few inches—and enabled us to have communication with these—as they proved to be— extremely bad natives, because this communication enabled us—or rather myself, as none of the rest of the whites knew the slightest about it or hardly anything else—to take a fresh departure, by showing us the position we were in, in regard to our future destination. We dropped our stone "kellick," or anchor, in about four feet of water, taking the precaution not to, at first, approach these strange natives too boldly, opposite a village, situated above high-water mark, where we could see some of the huts nestling among the banana trees, under the tall coco-palms in this truly picturesque locality.

The natives—i.e. all the males—were down at the water's edge, evidently waiting to receive us, as they had seen us approaching for the last half-hour. They were all armed—a good few of them with muskets—the rest with native implements of war, and some with tomahawks. This I thought very little of, as it was the custom in those times hardly to leave their doorways unarmed, but no females being mixed with them on the beach, this latter circumstance looked to me somewhat suspicious! I could not see a single solitary canoe, either in the water or hauled up on the beach, and the job I had imposed upon myself I did not half like—having to communicate with these natives—and yet, if I did not exactly think, I *hoped* that my fears were groundless. I selected the largest root of "yagone" we had brought from Fortuna and lowered myself into the water, which was well above my middle, and then desired the root of grog to be placed upon my shoulders, leaving word not to shift the canoe, without my orders, and if they saw me knocked over, they were to shoot as many of my murderers as they could, and then take care of themselves the best way they could, but not to be uselessly parading the muskets. They said, "God forbid that it should come to that!" I told them the last thing to let the loaded muskets remain under the rug which had been covered over them until really required, and then proceeded to the shore with my shoulder-load.

Immediately I began to rise the dry beach I lowered the root from my shoulder so as not to be conveying it along above, as it were, their heads, as they sat squatting just ahead of me. I also saluted, not only themselves, but their very beach with the respectful "dwa woah" as I approached them, stooping as is the custom, delivered my speech to the following effect. I represented that we had been living on Fortuna with Sam, the king, and that he had sent that *"yagone levu"* as a token and confirmation to the king of Lomaloma of his respects, hoping that he would receive and protect his white sons, till he should be able to return the obligation at some future, and he hoped at no distant period. They accepted it, but in a very cold manner, accompanied with a low-life, blackguard grin! The man who received it—a splendid specimen of a savage—large-sized, well-whiskered and moustached, smooth-skinned, and about thirty years of age. He was armed with a very large, broad-headed battle-axe, and as bright as silver, conspicuously contrasting with its elaborately carved and highly polished ebony handle, which was also further ornamented

CANNIBAL JACK

with various coloured sennet, answering the useful as well as ornamental purpose of preventing his grasp from slipping when in the act of using it in the bloody purposes which it was intended for!

This man's bearing was quite in keeping with his formidable weapon; for, although exceedingly handsome as a *tout ensemble,* he had an extremely sinister and supercilious look, and no wonder, seeing that he was a murderer and cannibal of the first water! He stood up over me, tapping me on the shoulder, telling me that "the name of that island was Cikobia off the Macuaca coast—(there being two Cikobias in the country) and not Lomaloma at all!" conveying to me that I had made a mistake, and a very great one too! The people all bursting out in a very derisive laugh, my heart, for the moment, was in my mouth, but I did not betray the slightest fear in my countenance, I having well schooled myself, for years past, in acts of diplomacy, and had long since learned to disguise my thoughts, by having full command over both my language and expression.

I instinctively found my hand making towards my formidable sheath-knife, which had never left me since I had recovered it, after being hung up by the heels, before related! I corrected the impulse without being observed, and then made answer in that very bland voice, which I so well knew how to assume in all emergencies which required that particular touch, telling him that in that case, I was extremely and agreeably surprised in two ways; one, on account of the claim I had on their hospitality, through my father Bonavidogo, the Macuaca prince, and, besides, I knew from common report, so much so indeed, that it had become quite proverbial, that the Cikobia chiefs (gentlemen) were the noblest race in Fiji, in respect to magnanimity, etc., adding, that I would now repair to the canoe and escort the white men on shore, as they would be highly rejoiced to learn that I had fallen in with such great gentlemen ("Turagas"). I went, without any objections on their part, they thinking, no doubt, that that plan would be the best and least trouble in securing the whole of us for the oven! When I was about a third of the way to the canoe—she being not more than 300 yards from the shore—another horse-laugh grated most hideously disagreeably on my ears from these determined cannibals, at some of their brutal jokes at having trapped so easily, no doubt, and also at the extreme softness of my character, having taken my *pretended* bland confidence in the grossness of their intellects, for ingenuousness.

A couple of fellows followed me with a tomahawk each. I gave these natives a piece of damper each, eating a piece myself to allay their suspicion respecting poison—a thing, they, among other qualifications, are extremely expert at administrating. I now told the Yankees to be quite deliberate and cool, with no bustle, excitement or fear, but do exactly as I told them, and see the two sails quite clear for spreeting, one at each, and the third one in readiness to lift the stone anchor, simultaneously with spreeting the sails, when I gave the order, adding, that if any mistake was made that it was quite sure and certain that we should all be cooked and eaten, because this was the notorious Cikobia, whose inhabitants had not more than eighteen months or two years before, slaughtered and devoured some thirty or forty Tongans, who had drifted from some of the Friendly Islands to the eastward, and that the rest I would tell them when we were clear, because there was not time now, but to business at once, when I let out a shout and the anchor was up and the sails spreeted in about three seconds, but the two savages still held on to the canoe and prevented her going ahead, although the sails were both full, I having hauled the sheets aft, when I immediately hauled a loaded musket from under the rug, full cocked it, and presented it first at one and then at the other savage's head,. and actually shoved the muzzle hard against their faces swearing in a very loud and savage voice, in the Fiji language, if they did not let go I would eat their brains! which being put into its original is, *"Laiva na waga agau moiya!"* And they did let go, and the canoe forged ahead at once, and at the same time we received the fire from the whole of the muskets of the savages on the beach, nine of the balls passing through our two sails, leaving the holes as clean cut as though clipped with a pair of scissors, and how in the devil they got through without first going through some, at any rate, of our bodies I could not make out, as the sails were purposely made with very little hoist for the safety of the vessel, coming down flush with the deck.

The Yankees now retaliated by firing their three muskets right in among the natives, but without any marked effect, the canoe being too far off, as she was now going through the water at the rate of knots. Seeing this, in my excitement, I called out, "why the hell! did you not fire at the two savages, who are closer to, and who have been doing their utmost to detain the canoe in order to get us cooked!" letting strip myself with my undischarged musket, and breaking the backbone of one of these vermin, who had made so cock-sure of having white men's flesh for supper. He fell forward on his face in the water, and so, after getting a feed of hard damper in front, and hard ball behind, from me, I thought, and said, he ought to have been well satisfied, seeing that nothing more could be done for him, unless we secured his body, and served it in the same way as they had intended serving ours, i.e. eating it! I called out to his escaped companion, telling him to go on shore and look out for me at some future time, and to tell his townies that I would have further satisfaction if it took a lifetime to accomplish!

And now, as we were quite clear, I had ample time to explain to my canoe mates, in answer to their incessant questions, the cause of the mistake we had fallen into respecting the reckoning. I said that I had, in the first place, laid out to make Lomaloma, which was quite fifty miles further to windward, where I was sure that landing was safe

in regard to the inhabitants, because a number of
Tongans resided there, but as I had kept the canoe off
two points, for the sake of expediting her pace
through the bad weather, which I hourly expected
and dreaded, besides the soundness of the bottom
of these kinds of crafts, but that I was now opposite
the part which I wished to make, and that I now
knew exactly where we were. I proposed that we
should return thanks again to the merciful Providence which had so miraculously saved us, and especially in the case of the musket balls, the holes of
which in the sails were just as high from the deck
as our heads and breasts, and so I could only account
for this inexplicable enigma by miraculous inter-
position! We therefore acknowledged *that* in few
words, beseeching His further aid to see that we arrived safe and sound at the place we were now steering for—the entrance of Neteva Bay. I also asked
forgiveness for my somewhat rash act in taking a
fellow-creature's life, which did not sit easy, by any
means, on my conscience, seeing that my life was in
no danger from this particular benighted savage,
and although he fully deserved death for the conniv-
ing for the destruction of ours, according to human
reasoning, yet there was an inward, small voice,

which told, that at the last and final tribunal, in that awful day, that a different construction *might* be put on it for my wantonness, and I fully repented me that I had been his executioner!

The reader may be tempted to think, and even ask, how I knew, in the first place, that they really intended to take our lives at all? and whether it might not have been all the effect of fear which brought me to this conclusion? Let me ask and tell this sagacious reader, Who was likely to be the best judge, he or I, in the matter? My conscience is quite clear on this head, because I heard with my own ears, whilst the savage, and who, no doubt, was the chief, so significantly tapped me twice on the shoulder, whilst he stood over me with his battle-axe —in my helpless condition, the other natives make allusion to the "lovo" (oven) and the Tongans, coupling "Vavalaga" (white men) as being in the same predicament as the former unfortunate victims, boastfully and gloatingly exulting on their prowess, and besides, like any other ferocious and voracious beasts, they had had a taste of blood, and so their appetites were whetted!

We now took a good feed of damper, pork, and beef—the former being as sweet as when first baked, and would have kept so, I believe, for a week longer, in consequence of having no leaven in it. We then had about a dozen of the young coco-nuts, and which would have also kept perhaps a couple of weeks longer, on account of not being denuded of their outer skins. We washed all down by the usual half-pint of diluted "samshu" and prepared to be out all night. The wind shifted and blew like Old Harry, but, fortunately, it was still fair, and even fairer than usual, and wishing to take advantage of it, we goose-winged our sails, and carried on all top ropes, the vine-rigging being extremely strong. We all got aft so as to put her well by the stern, cocking the head out of the water somewhat. It now took two of us to steer through this, to us, formidable sea, the other two bailing all they knew! But still we held out, and at daylight we found ourselves right opposite the entrance of Neteva Bay. We could have gone into Naviu as Udu Point bore well off our starboard bow, but as I was far from certain how politics stood, or what changes had taken place during my absence of something considerably over a year in this very changing part of this very change-able country, I thought it more prudent to run no risks, and so kept her going, keeping more over to the port-hand of the bay, keeping well in shore lest anything *might,* now that we were so near our destination, happen to our frail craft. We were now in a fair way of reaching Neteva in safety, perhaps half-way down this very deep bay, or more properly, perhaps, frith or estuary.

And now whilst the canoe is skimming along over the great deal smoother surface of the sea than it was outside the bay during the past night, let me pause to relate that, notwithstanding the fact that I had been killed outright some half-dozen times in these Fiji Islands—it being a mere matter of arithmetic only, inasmuch as I had been half-killed more than, or at any rate, quite a dozen times already, and as twelve halves are six wholes all the world over, so that apparent misnomer is easily accounted for. There was a fascination in this kind of life, not only in the youthful and green portion of it, but lasting into and through the yellow and sere; and even now that I am verging on the allotted period, according to the Bible theory, of threescore and ten, and that if the frosts and snows of the frigid or even temperate zones had very little to do towards contributing to the flour-bag appearance of the hair of my head and beard, which Old

CANNIBAL JACK

Father Time has so industriously shaken over me even in the torrid zone—I say I still have a yearning, even at this age, for the sweets of that exhilarating, wild, natural life, so distinct from the artificial, craving, envious, selfish, and greedy life of civilization! And, no doubt, I have been happier in following the bent of my inclinations than I should have been in following any other or more forced pursuits. I was no sooner out of one scrape than I longed to be into another. And the freedom of this canoe sailing for instance—the frailer the craft, the more buoyant I always felt, and especially if I was the leader in these, what other people would have termed hare-brained and wild-goose chases! The elasticity of spirits which I experienced, as I had hundreds of times before, and thousands of times since, even upon this very trivial occasion, whilst we were flying over the water, the picturesque shore receding like lightning as we glided so noiselessly along, not being more than half a mile distant at any time, sometimes much less—Neteva just ahead of us.

CANNIBAL JACK

A ND now we arrived at Neteva Beach, where there were a number of natives fishing, and which occupation they immediately dropped when they recognized me amongst the rest of the whites, in order to greet us and escort us into the town, situated a short half-hour's walk inland, carrying everything which was movable with them excepting the freshwater and the stone anchor—the former, after taking a drink to test the taste of foreign water, they poured out, the latter they secreted in the bushes for the time being, till a better opportunity offered for conveying it into the town, where it would become a kind of pillar opposite some of the heathen temples, and where it would also become, no doubt, the site for immolating some yet unborn infants to the bloody gods by dashing their brains out upon it! Such is life—heathen life—and such is death!

As we proceeded on towards the town, they apprised me of the fact that I was now the father of two children—the first, they thought, that I had ever fathered—one a boy, the other a girl, the boy being a "vasu" to Taniloa, the girl by the Rotuma woman. At this news I called a halt, and we all sat down by the side-path and took a good stiff bout of the samshu, wishing luck to these two youngsters, and as there was something left after we whites had imbibed, I insisted that the natives should drink the healths of my children, and which they did, not, however, without considerable wincing, it being the first time they had tasted alcohol, and, it is to be hoped, the last. I then gave them the remains of the cut damper, reserving one whole one for the women; but when they got to the beef, they asked if it was "baola"! and I had some difficulty in making them believe that it was "bulamakau" (beef), because though the name of oxen was quite familiar, yet they had never even seen one of these animals.

The three Americans and myself then dressed ourselves in the print which still remained for the purpose, as well as for my wives. We wound it round our bodies in the form which the natives with their home-made tappa or "masi" adopt after having been absent in a distant part of the country for any length of time, and then strip themselves by simply turning round and round and presenting it to their friends and called "so levu lailai" (small fair). We did the same, presenting it to Bonavidogo, as a rejoicing offering on account of our again meeting after my longish absence. It and the four muskets were duly received and thanked for in the usual style, calling the Neteva Gods to witness that I and my white friends were heartily welcome, and the Fortuna "yagone" was masticated, mixed, and discussed. After this, a return present, in the shape of a feast, was appointed to be held in my honour after the lapse of three days.

I then took up the last remaining root of Fortuna grog to the old king—the brother of Bonavidogo's mother, and who had long since been dead, and which deceased "marama" (lady or queen) was the source of all Bonavidogo's greatness in this place, as well as all its tributaries. This old man, who was nearly white in body on account of being almost entirely confined to his "big-house" or palace, occasioned by his extreme fatness—weighing perhaps nearer twenty-five than twenty stone—and was called "Turaga davo" (reclining king).

The old man was extremely delighted at my safe return, squeezing and hugging me within an inch of my life, his long finger-nails—quite an inch long —penetrating almost through my shirt and into my skin, with unfeigned rejoicing, the tears streaming down the furrows of his aged cheeks! We had a drink of "yagone" together and then a "wase" after it, there being no difficulty about the latter in this house because some score or more of large and small earthen pots were incessantly kept going day and night—and perhaps had been for quite forty or fifty years past in the same way. There was always pork, fish, fowl, and turtle on hand at a minute's warning, besides vegetables of every description, and all the luxuries of the land arriving from far and near every day—hence, perhaps, his big corporation! and yet he was not a big eater, a couple or three mouthfuls generally sufficing, but then he ate quite twenty times a day, and that of the very best. He was really and truly a *bon-vivant,* not eating to live but living to eat, and that incessantly up to twelve o'clock at night every night of his life. One could hear the incessant hand-clapping of all the inmates of that house—amounting to quite fifty persons—mostly of the feminine gender—indicating that the "Turaga davo's" appetite was for the time being appeased!

After giving him a couple of fathoms of double-width sheeting, the best thing I could think of as a present, the old fellow wanting for nothing in this world, and which I thought would answer well to keep the flies from his extremely fat carcass, whilst taking his accustomed long daily siesta, and which would, at the same time, greatly relieve his wives, concubines, daughters, granddaughters, great-granddaughters, servants, slaves, adopted sons and daughters, *et hoc genus omne,* from the incessant drudgery of fanning off these pestering annoyances, the flies. I say, after making him this present, I retired, and now I repaired to the residence of my four wives, all of whom I found well and hearty and very happy at my return—telling me that they had almost given me up, all showing me—excepting the Rotuma woman—that they had amputated the little finger of each of their left hands as a "loloku" (mourning) for my long absence! My "bobula" (slave) was equally rejoiced at my return, telling me that through his dissuasion my wives were still alive, because they had several times prepared to sacrifice their lives by strangling at once; in particular he had actually deterred the three Fiji women by main force from their fell purpose of self-immolation in sacrifice to my manes, believing —and nobody could convince them to the contrary —that I was dead, voluntarily retiring into the "atu" (bush) for that purpose, and he said that he was now "cegu" (?) (relieved) because he had been re-

85

duced to almost complete exhaustion watching lest they should renew the attempt!

Notwithstanding all this requisite vigilance in my behalf, he had managed to put in a large plantation of yams with the women's assistance in my absence, and which were now at maturity, and although not yet dedicated to the "god of plenty," in common with all the people's annats or first fruits, he dug some up for me to eat, saying the gods could wait!—a thing often winked at in the case of high personages! and who so high a personage, in this faithful fellow's estimation, as myself?

I now had time to caress my two children; the girl eight months old and as nigh white as d——n it, her mother being an extremely light-coloured woman, even for a "kanaka"—that breed being more akin to the white race than the black, and a devilish lot better looking than the generality of either; the boy, a fine child for his age—seven months—but something darker than the girl in consequence of his mother being Fiji. They already began proposing to carrying him to Tuneloa for his grandfather and grandmother to see, and also to initiate him into having those two old people's pigs killed on the strength of his "vasu"-ship to the family, just merely by holding the child's hand up and pointing it to these old people's pigs, when they would be immediately slaughtered and dressed ready for the oven, according to the custom of the country. The Rotuma woman's child, being a female, stood for not much account, even had she been the daughter of a Fiji woman, to say nothing of the mother being foreign, and where "vasu"-ship is unknown—different countries, different fashions—and so with different islands, especially when inhabited by different races, even if not so very far off.

This "vasu" business is all powerful, and especially when the vasu is the son of a chief by the sister of a chief of another place; and when on a visit to his uncle's territories, he generally causes great havoc, and especially amongst the live stock, because he is not only entitled to seize property of every description from the whole of his mother's blood-relations, but also from every family—high or low, which his uncle rules—supposing the latter is the head chief—a common vasu by a common woman can only take from *her* family.

CANNIBAL JACK

I now have to make a jump, as it were, over a few years of my autobiography, which I have written on nineteen common copy-books, and which is carried up to the twenty-sixth year of my age—the preceding part of this manuscript being the contents of one copy-book only, and that the ninth one, because I numbered each one as I commenced it. I propose copying off the sixteenth and seventeenth, which will just about fill up this blank book, but then, by this plan, of course the consecutive order of the narrative will be considerably interrupted, and perhaps somewhat marred, because I cannot stop to explain so minutely in these extracts as I have done throughout the main work as I proceeded. I have still forty-four years of "my life" unwritten, and which long period has been fraught with quite as much adventure as the preceding twenty-six years —I being now in my seventieth year.

The difficulty with the reader of these extracts will be when I refer to some passages which are in the main body of the autobiography, and not in the extracts, to comprehend what I allude to; but as this is a mere specimen of the whole, and which will be for sale, providing this is accepted and reasonably paid for, but if rejected as no use to other people, I fully depend on the honour of the peruser in having it returned, as it will be still of some importance to myself, *Cannibal Jack.*

No. 16

THIS island of Taviuni—the third in size in the Fiji group, after the two big lands of Viti Levu and Vanua Levu.—It has often been termed the "Garden of Fiji" in respect to prolificness, importance, etc., etc., and as I am about to leave it, perhaps for ever, I may as well mention, *en passant,* that it is a high, mountainous (and of volcanic formation) one, with a large lake in its middle—no doubt, the extinct crater of a former volcano, perhaps some thousands of years old, nay, tens of thousands, who can tell? The natives say that the lake is exceedingly deep, even bottomless; but then, we may take this for what it is worth, in the same way as we take the story they tell and believe, even in these late comparatively enlightened times, about sows having pigs even if they have been kept in a sty all their lives separate from the boars! also, that a mare, when she foals, always brings forth a lion!

89

So persistent are they, not only in their superstitious nonsense, but also in the preconsidered foolish notions of the old heathen times, that it will take generations before they are all completely eradicated.

The island is full of a smallish, indigenous, hard yam, called "tivoli," very nutritious and staying as food, so that it would be next to impossible for the aborigines to starve, even if they should neglect planting altogether. They have in other parts of Fiji, and in many parts, another kind of wild yam, called "tikau," but this kind is of an immense size —white, soft, palatable, and nutritious. I have frequently seen the larger ones, quite six feet long, upwards of two feet in circumference and weighing quite a hundred pounds.

There is another chief town on this island besides Somosomo, called Vuna, but it derives its importance from a spiritual point of view—its inhabitants being acknowledged by their neighbours, far and near, to have descended from the gods. God bless them! but this "fact" (?) does not prevent them being attacked by their enemies, carried away into slavery, and sometimes killed and eaten!

There is also another large town with its tributaries on the opposite side of the island. But Somosomo with its Tuecakau dynasty was always considered the capital of Taviuni. This savage city —the inhabitants of which were exceedingly "flash" —had several peculiarities—one of which was the habit they adopted when Tuecakau, the king, had imbibed his morning dish of "yagone"—always about half-past 7 a.m.—to screech and halloo aloud from house to house, inside and outside, echoing, and re-echoing all over the place, till at last it became—to me at least—perfectly disgusting. This screeching was called "kaila."

They had this same practice of kaila whenever any of the Bau fleets appeared in sight in the offing from to leeward, and for which they always maintained a constant look out from the top of a hill hard-by; and one forenoon this screeching was heard from far and near, and as it was some time past the accustomed time of Tuecakau's drinking bout, and I having been some time previous to this apprised of the formidable Cakobau being on the look out for reprisals on us whites for having so signally thwarted him in his fell intent of torturing us under the new mode, and devouring us afterwards, besides knowing from good authority that C. Pickering had some time since been obliged to flee the country, by taking himself off to Fortuna, and there remain till such time as things quieted down somewhat in Fiji. And there he did remain till he had buried his head wife—the mother of his first-born half-caste child; but afterwards he returned again, and then, from first to last, he had born to him as many as a dozen half-caste children, by different mothers, most of whom turned out very well—the girls marrying whites of prominence, as the country was now undergoing a change for the better—the boys, now well sprinkled with grey—1888—becoming carpenters, etc., etc.; the carpenter portion of them turning out vessels quite as good and in as short a time as white carpenters, and then sailing them in quite if not better style, and especially in regard of keeping them clear of the reefs, they being quite *au fait* in the geography of the country, and often beating the whites in the yearly regattas. And now these again have large families, their grown-up daughters, and even granddaughters being quite eligible partners for whites, and somewhat sought for, but generally unsuccessfully, they being, by nature, gregarious, and do not easily amalgamate, but rather prefer their own breed—

half-caste to half-caste. The male half-caste some-times take full-blooded Fijian women for wives, but never, as yet, white women. Pure Fijian males hardly ever get a half-caste wife—not that the lat-ter would object for a moment, were it not for the excessively selfish clannishness of the half-caste masculine gender in this particular and hardly in any other. The most of them are inclined to im-bibe ardent spirits, and were it not for the present restrictions I shudder to think what would follow! They number now (1889) perhaps, at a rough esti-mate—my own estimate, and which is a mere guess —men, women, and children—from four to five hundred—perhaps 1,000.

But to return, I say, as this "kaila" screeching was being performed so extensively all through the place, and the refrain being taken up on all sides by men, women and children, and as it was long past the early part of the morning when Tuecakau's accus-tomed portion of this ridiculous piece of "flash" was always performed, I had not the slightest doubt that it was the Bau fleet, and as it was more than imperative on me to increase the distance between these now fast approaching gentry and myself, and as Tuecakau had, quite opportunely, a favourite wife lying at death's door, and all for the want (I *said*) of medicine—the missionary, or missionaries rather—there being two—having some time past, after expending £7,000, I was told by good authority, shaken the dust from their feet and retired from this most incorrigible place!

I hastened to this autocrat—autocrat in the most extended meaning of the word—making a virtue of a most (to me) imperative necessity, and proposed that a fast-sailing "tambelai" canoe, should immediately be got ready—ere too late—and despatch me off to Lekeba to get medicine from Dr. Lythe— the missionary of that place. This proposition of mine was immediately gratefully (apparently) acceded to, and so just as the Bau fleet were coming in, I was going out, and a lucky job for myself, before the Bau devils had an opportunity of learning that I was within a hundred miles of the vicinity, which these would-be smart fellows in their thickheadedness supposed, or else I should have been going out of existence quicker than I could have said Jack Robinson, instead of the passage!

We went from island to island, as there was no immediate danger of this lady; in fact, to tell the honest truth, there was nothing more the matter with her than that she wished to gain a greater share of that caressing (which, in this country, is so infinitesimally divided among numerous recipients) from her lord and master—Tuecakau (N.B. the "c" is sounded as "thar"), and knowing, with the instinct of her sex, that the more languid she appeared to be, the more interesting she would become! In calling at these islands—the crew nothing loth— as by this plan the feasting hinged—I had an opportunity of converting all my muskets—which had been hastily put on board—into tortoiseshell. Of course we slept each night at a separate island—the crew, as usual again, nothing loth, I being, in their estimation, the only responsible personage on board.

We eventually reached Lekeba, when I hurried up to Dr. Lythe and secured a small bottle of castor-oil and a tablespoon, when I despatched the canoe back again with a fair wind, with orders to administer a tablespoon of this assuaging medicament, whenever her languid ladyship was inclined to be costive, and not without, strictly inculcating that she was not to be restricted—as is their foolish wont—to certain innutritious food, but to ply her with all manner of soups—and especially those made from fowls, plenty of young coco-nuts, etc., etc. I also sent my love to

the two wives I had lately acquired from Tuecakau, with strict injunctions that they were not to
take to themselves other husbands—at any rate, not
till they again heard from me—a thing, poor devils,
they would have had a long time to wait for, because, it so happened, that in a very few months—
after making several ineffectual trials—I was clean
out of Fiji and did not return again for nineteen
years, but this was a thing I could not, at the time,
foresee, but had to work as circumstances dictated,
and as they cropped up! The reader may possibly
think that he would have acted differently, without
considering, for a moment, that we are emphatically
"children of circumstances," and especially in those
cannibal countries and those very trying times. I
was but too grateful for my head being allowed to
remain upon my shoulders, without troubling myself very much about comparative trivialities, and so
would he have been, that is, if he had had the gift
of self-preservation as strongly developed in his nod-
dle as I fancy it is in that humble servant, Cannibal
Jack's sagacious reader.

CANNIBAL JACK

I T will be remembered by the reader—now just a twelve-month ago—that in leaving Lekeba, that I had demolished with my tomahawk the old chief Lua's fancy little boat, and his arm-chest, besides the little natty pearl fish-boxes, which I had with such infinite trouble constructed for him out on the Island of Ogea, just previous to me embarking on board the murdering Butoni chief's canoe for my trip to leeward. Since that, I had learned, from good authority, that he had threatened to throw his religion up for the sake of murdering me the minute he again clapped his eyes upon me!

After I had despatched the canoe with the languid beauty's medicine to leeward, I went into an old white man's house, who was now living in the settlement on the Lekeba Beach among the Tongans, and whilst shaking hands with him as an old acquaintance, a messenger arrived begging gun-flints for Lua, because he now stood in great need of those articles, he expecting every day the long-threatened besieging attack upon this fortified town of "Wacewace" (Wathewathe) by Vuetasau, the king's brother of Tubo—the capital of Lekeba.

This old white man had no flints, or anything else, —in fact, he being extremely poor, as many other unfortunate whites have been and are to this day in these South Seas. I laid hold of this boy-messenger, and compelled him to follow me up to Mr. Calvert's—the fellow missionary on this station of Dr. Lythe's—where I had left my two chests just a year before for safe keeping, whilst I took my trip to the "leeward," and lucky for me that I was back again within a day or two of the prescribed time, or else Bob, the Yankee, who had been the year before "thirty-two or forty-two years old"—he could not be certain which, but he was sure there was a two in it in either case!—would have owned the chest, with all their contents. I speedily, after getting the keys from Mr. Calvert, opened the one with the "small trade" in it, the other containing my tools only, and extracted a couple of dozen new gun-flints, putting a dozen in each of my trousers pockets, and straightway proceeded with the boy to Lua's fortified town of Wacewace.

When we arrived opposite the moat—and which we did in something less than an hour—I saluted the place with the usual friendly "dwar waah," and the slip-logs were immediately withdrawn, and in another minute I stood in the presence of Lua himself in his big house, and turning both pockets inside out with both my hands—one in each—letting the flints drop on the mats at my feet opposite him, saying in a loud and cheerful voice, "The friend in need is the friend indeed," adding his favourite facetious exclamation of *"Chekoli!"*, when the old warrior raked the flints together, and then nosed me in the usual mode of salutation among relations after a prolonged absence. I felt the tears from the eyes of this veteran as he hugged me, but he soon dried them, adding the hearty *"Chikoli!"* when all animosity was at an end. I never thought of making the most distant allusion to the murderous threat he had used towards me, and he, no doubt, thought I had never heard of it. And he returned the compliment by making no allusion whatever to the demolishing by the tomahawk of the things which he had at the first made so cock-sure of receiving from me. And now he invited me to stay with him at Wacewace altogether, in order to keep the company of his most beautiful little daughter—a girl of about fifteen—and, as a further inducement, added, that I should thereby shortly have an opportunity of gratifying my natural propensity in shooting "bukolas," and so killing two birds with one stone—the second and principal bird being the defence of Tupo—the girl's name.

We had not long to wait, for in less than a week after this the long expected besieging business came off. One morning they came along from Tubo, headed by Vuetasau, Tuniau's brother. These kings' brothers are generally at the head of all the mischief which is so frequently happening at all the islands, and at all parts of the islands, and often simultaneously, so that the whole of the country, or rather its inhabitants are stirred up into a perpetual turmoil, the complications of which are almost impossible to conceive, thereby rendering the paths almost impassable, as well as extremely dangerous to travel, and which facts account for that gregariousness which so universally obtains, and which, at the first blush of the thing, looks in the eyes of a foreigner so preposterously absurd—at least it, at first sight, looked so to me,—and I used to think their perpetually being armed was a piece of ostentation merely; but I soon learned to think differently and estimate the custom at its proper value, not, however, before I had been (as near as two farthings are to a halfpenny), upon more than one occasion, nearly potted for my temerity! These brothers ar-

CANNIBAL JACK

rogate to themselves great authority, and are by the greatest difficulty restrained by their older brethren, who are, as a general thing, quieter people.

It happened that the whole of the people of Wace-wace were absent in their gardens this very morning—they having waited considerably over a month for this threatened siege—excepting Lua, his wife (Tuniau's daughter) and myself. They did not approach very boldly, but one fellow was seen within a yard or two of the outer edge of the moat, sheltering himself behind a breadfruit-tree, and as it was evident to all three of us for what purpose he was there, Lua insisted that he should be shot. The tree barely covered his body. Lua fired one barrel of his double-barrelled piece, grazing the bark of the tree, when the native exposed his head on its other side, and Lua, being a dead shot, passed a ball completely through the skull of this unlucky savage! And now this drew on the rest of them who had witnessed the whole of the performance, albeit not one of them had been hitherto seen by us, they being so completely hidden by the scrub, long grass, etc. They came along screeching their unearthly yells, the sound of which is really terrific! They took about two seconds to secure the body of their comrade, we peppering away at them in the meantime, not for the sake of eating it, albeit they were heathens and cannibals, but for the interment, he being a towney. They fired all their muskets at us, we being obliged to somewhat expose our heads above the embankment in order to see what was going on. They crossed the moat and rushed up the embankment in great style, but as the foremost three or four were shot dead, just as they were about to jump into the town, from the top of the rampart, we both being as busy as ever we were able discharging, whilst that brave as well as beautiful woman Tuniau's daughter, Lua's wife, was reloading the muskets, double-barrelled pieces, etc., and handing them to us with twice the coolness that either of us men possessed, we being both of us of very excitable temperaments; but this very excitement, no doubt, proved the salvation of the place, as it kept us from collapsing; but there was nothing to boast of, for we all ran a very narrow squeak of our lives, and had the savages known there were but two defending the place, instead of scores, as they thought, and as they told us afterwards, I should not now be scribbling its account! They also told us that they accounted for the profound silence which was being so religiously maintained within the town, and so contrary to the universal uproar and defiant screeching challenges which almost always prevails upon all these occasions, as a mere ruse to blind and draw them on to their destruction, and seeing that there was a white man with the besieged, they naturally concluded that there was some mystery about the affair, and that it would be rashness indeed to prosecute the siege in defiance of these palpable albeit silent admonitions—hence their precipitate retreat before they were entrapped in some new-fangled stratagem, organized by a "Vavalaga" (foreigner) and from which it would be impossible to extricate themselves! They did not *dream,* for an instant, that there were no people at all, hardly, in the town, to make the accustomed noise even if required!

They retired in as good order, and as briskly as they could, seeing that our shots were following them to the last moment, as long as a soul was in sight, carrying off their dead and wounded—a couple or three only of the latter, if I rightly remember at this great distance of time.

The next day at about eleven o'clock Vuetasau came along with about three or four followers at the most, and saluted the town with the usual respectful "duar waar"—a very different salutation from that of the day before, when it had been all abuse!—when he was immediately admitted through the draw-logs, which had been removed for that purpose, and as quickly closed again, in case of treachery!

He had with him a bunch of whales' teeth, which were duly presented with the accompanying speech, to the effect that it was human nature to fall out, and human nature to fall in again, and the fortune of war, sometimes to beat, at other times to be beaten! These were accepted by Lua with an appropriate thanksgiving speech to the great protecting Jehova, who had so mercifully saved his life from the hands of powerful but gallant enemies, and that it was all owing to his being a Christian, although an unworthy one, he said, adding his particular and favourite "Jikoli!" which had originated, I almost think, in the first place, from this jolly old dog himself,—at any rate, it was oftener in his mouth than anyone else's.

It was generally believed that Tuniau the king had been instigating his brother Vuetasau, in that covert way so peculiar to Fijians, to besiege Wace-wace, so that he should get shot and rendered there-

CANNIBAL JACK

by perfectly harmless for the future to himself. But in this intention, if true, and no doubt it was, he miserably failed, for Vuetasau took precious good care to keep out of the way of all danger, when it came to the deciding point, leaving his poor followers—the order of the march being quite reversed by he himself becoming follower when it came to the breach—to stand all the brunt. And which is generally the case with most of the chiefs throughout the group, excepting such men as Cakobau, Ratu Quara, Bonavidogo, and a few others.

And now that peace was restored, the conquerors and conquered were eating and drinking together as though nothing unusual had ever happened, to say nothing of the recentness as well as seriousness of this little episode—in fact they were heartily laughing at the foolishness, and even awkwardness of the braver portion of these unfortunate fellows who had licked the dust!

Old Lua, as soon as Tupo, his daughter, returned from the distant gardens with the rest of the inhabitants, insisted that she should kiss me as a tribute of gratitude for the assistance I had rendered in defending the place, and which she did with considerable coyness, as she dare not disregard her father's orders. He then said, that that was an earnest of a thousand others, and now that I had it all in my own hands, as he there and then gave his permission before her mother, and who was of the same mind as himself, the quicker I brought it to a conclusion by taking her to Mr. Calvert and getting married the better it would be for all parties and especially for herself, before she had an opportunity—like her older sister "Matai ika" (Fisheye)—of going to the bad, but "woe be to the lad who should dare without his consent to aspire to the hand of *Lua's* daughter! her sister's case being an exception, and quite beyond his control, as it happened in Bau, and by Cakobau himself, whilst on a visit to that exceedingly immoral place!" "And the quicker I consummated this little job the better it would be for myself, for I should by that means secure to myself a permanent good figure of a wife, because if made a wife of when quite a child the certainty of becoming too corpulent afterwards— which all females with any Tongan blood in them were very liable to—would be obviated."

But instead of marrying in the Christian style— a thing I must confess seldom entered my head, seeing there were so many other ways of acquiring wives open to me, and as I had now on hand in different parts of the group six *bona fide* wives, and that it was quite imperative that I should seek safety for myself in increasing my distance from the biggest man in Fiji, and now my inveterate enemy, and more especially as I was painfully aware that I was as much in Cakobau's power here in Lekeba as though I had been nearly 100 miles nearer Bau, because Kamaeese, *alias* Mara, the "Vasu Levu" to the first mentioned of these two far apart places, was incessantly coming up from the latter, periodically, for the sake of collecting tribute from the former, as well as from all its somewhat numerous dependent islands, and conveying it down to the seat of government to leeward—Bau. I therefore, all at once, as it were, made up my mind that I would leave Fiji, if not altogether, for a time at any rate.

THERE was a large new canoe just completed, which had been built in Fiji by Tongan carpenters as was their wont in those times—Tonga not being equally famous like the "lau" (weather islands) of Fiji for large timber. These canoes were regularly constructed of large planking, a matter of quite two inches thick when the canoe was of the largest size and intended to carry nearly and sometimes quite one hundred people. Inside of each of these plankings a stout ridge was left on the upper and lower edge for the purpose of being pierced with almost innumerable holes in close contact with each other, and strong sennit made from the coconut fibre passed through these holes on the upper edge of the last plank into the opposite holes directly above on the lower edge of the next plank, and so on, till finished; there were also left at intervals stout ridges across each plank, for the sake of adding strength. In no case did they ever get more than two planks from a log, however large, as they always divided it into two pieces longitudinally with axes—pit saws being a thing unknown—and they then dubbed the round parts of these immense slabs away, leaving nothing but the heart of the timber for their use. And after all this was completed, before laying the beams which answered a double purpose, the one for holding the two canoes together —as I am endeavouring to describe a *double* canoe —the other for laying the decks upon, the insides of both canoes were again strongly timbered, and shelves supported from side to side by these timbers

CANNIBAL JACK

for the purpose of stowing their baskets of provisions upon, clear of the bilge water in the hold, during a long voyage, and which they sometimes make to the extent of 600 or 800 or even 1,000 miles—being not infrequently absent a year or two from home, wandering and gadding about from island to island, going through all Samoa, Fiji, and all the "Friendly Islands," not omitting even the more distant ones of Wallis' Island, Fortuna, Nieuafou, Nieuatobu tabu, as well as the three nearer groups of Tongatabu, Vavao and Hapai.

The wood with which they build is wonderfully durable and susceptible of a high polish. They leave the outside of the canoes quite as smooth as an ordinary European vessel's sides. A certain particular one was pointed out to me as having been afloat—estimated by calculation and tradition combined—upwards of a century, and by diligent inquiring I found that this was no exaggeration—of course she had been relashed numbers of times and also repaired in different ways, time and again, but still a great many of her original planks were as sound as ever, and no wonder, as the wood is a species of teak and almost imperishable, and its Fiji name is "vesi."

CANNIBAL JACK

Respecting the sewings or lashings by the coconut fibre sennit, it is passed through and through some ten or a dozen times the opposite holes on each plank, that is, all along the protuberant ridges inside, left for that purpose, and the last turn or two being with difficulty and great strength of hand hauled through, and so completely filling up the holes, each part of the sennit being so arranged as to pass over and alongside the previous turns, so that it is impossible to shift, and forming little flat bulges, which are so neatly performed as to prove quite ornamental to the work, whilst being elaborated; and these bulges in hundreds, or even, perhaps, thousands, being so close together all along all the seams throughout the whole of the canoe inside, and of course out of sight when completed by being decked over, and I really believe that these parts, where the seams are, are much stronger than any other, the salt water tending to swell as well as preserve the lashings, so that it is next to impossible to leak, and I question whether that plan is not equal, if not even superior, to nail fastening, and especially if the nails are merely wrought instead of galvanized. It is quite equal, perhaps superior, to copper itself, for this kind of work.

CANNIBAL JACK

On board of this large new canoe, commanded as well as owned by one of the most eccentric men perhaps in the world—certainly one of the most eccentric in *this* part of the world—I embarked, she being bound for Tonga—the crew consisting of some forty or fifty Tongans who had been, some of them, four or five years, some less in Fiji. They were composed mostly of men, the rest women and children excepting some half-dozen mere lads, all desirous of returning to their own country, as the owner-chief himself also was, and especially as he wished to get his new vessel into his own country now that it was completed, after years of labour, he having all that time been obliged to come down to Fiji at almost regular stated periodical visits with property, tools, etc., to ply his carpenters with, besides presents for the Fiji chiefs for the care and trouble they had taken in supplying the mechanics with food, as well as seeing the logs duly hauled from the bush by their Fiji subjects—he (Finau) having made in all that long period, at least, a dozen trips for that purpose.

We started—the wind being fair—and which we had been waiting for.

We called and slept a couple of nights at Turtle

Island, native name "Vatoa," the last stage in Fiji,
and then made the last start for crossing the open
ocean—a distance of 300 miles—in order to reach
the Hapai group of the Friendly Islands; but, as we
had dallied in Fiji too long, our fair wind became
exhausted, died out altogether, and then shifted, coming dead ahead, and as it freshened and was too
strong to carry the whole of our *one* immense sail,
we were obliged to reduce it—a thing they do just
by hoisting up, a little way only, one of its corners
merely; and even if we could have carried the whole
of the sail, these canoes make but a poor fist at beating, notwithstanding the fact of their laying so close
to the wind, their bottoms being so very round and
smooth, drawing so very little water, and having no
keels, of course they drift, having no hold whatever
of the water, and so we put back when we were
closer to Tonga—that is, to the Hapais than Fiji.
We steered for Turtle Island again and the next
afternoon fetched it, but in the meantime I had
ample opportunity of witnessing some of the eccentricities, which were so universally ascribed to our
worthy captain—Ratu Finau! many of which had
been related to me by the youthful portion of our
crew, mostly for their own amusement, as well as a

CANNIBAL JACK

kindly hint to me not to be exposing myself by an exhibition of any of my own somewhat pronounced eccentricities in the presence of this "arch-demon" in regard to temper!

We were scudding away before the wind; the food had been baked in the flat sand and dirt-box for that purpose; the stones had been heated with no little difficulty as everything was more or less wet from the seas, which every now and again broke over us, we being not more than two feet and a half from the surface of the sea—in fact, the very largest of these canoes are never more than three feet out of the water; but, by dint of perseverance the food was baked, consisting of yams only, and shared out in the usual impartial manner—impartial, as a couple of natives sit back to back in contact with each other on the deck—one of them lifting a couple of pieces of yam—one in each hand, and then asks aloud, "Whose shall these be?" the other one answering in a loud voice, "They are for So-and-so!" mentioning the recipient's name without himself getting even a glimpse of each share, as there is sometimes a slight difference both in quality and size too, in spite of all care. We were going slower than the seas—going slow for the sake of safety, and so the

113

bailing had to be constantly attended to; but the natives began complaining about the drudgery of the thing—a thing there was not the slightest occasion for, seeing there were enough people and to spare both for steering and bailing too, providing they relieved each other in reasonable spells. Finau being somewhat out of sorts, no doubt, poor man, at the inauspicious turn things had taken, and the fact of his having to put back, and now hearing this dialogue from these contrary natives, and although he was a chief of some rank, yet none of these fellows actually belonged to him, and he thinking, no doubt, that that was the reason they took advantage by jangling in his presence.

This brought on the climax when he reached the holds, driving with the greatest impetuosity every soul out of them, seizing a bailer from the ablest-looking fellow's hand, ordering that not another soul on board the canoe should again enter one of the holds, for the purpose of bailing, and if anyone had the temerity to do so in defiance of his orders, that he did it at his peril! that he could and would bail the whole of the four holds himself and keep them dry too, and if he failed to do so the canoe might sink, and be d——d to her! and he would sink with her! She was his own and he could and would do as he liked with her, and if anyone offered the slightest demur against this decision, that he would there and then cut the lashings of the canoe and let her perish by drifting to piecemeal away, and then each one could take his choice, whether he swam for Tonga or Fiji, and if he did not like either alternative, he could swim to the hot place! "And now, you women, chew the grog and keep it going till we reach land, and give not a single soul a drop excepting the white man and myself!"

This most wonderful man, rushing from one hold to another, actually kept the whole of the four holds dry, bailing and drinking grog with superhuman strength and energy, and continued this most trying business for twenty-four consecutive hours without one moment's intermission or relaxation, not a soul daring to interfere by venturing to offer even the conciliatory property which is always done in all extreme cases, they all being too well acquainted with the idiosyncrasies of this more than hero's character, fearful lest they should make bad worse! I, being the favourite, ventured to help, but he mildly but firmly told me to desist! and so I continued to assist in the imbibing, or rather swilling, portion of the business only, and when we arrived at Vatoa I was heartily glad of it, because if the passage had lasted but a few hours longer, I, most undoubtedly, should have burst!

We arrived, as I said above, safe and sound, but now came the difficulty. We ran to leeward for shelter, and where the one and only settlement of this smallish island was situated; but as the wind was too strong to set the whole sail, and we could not get close enough to reach bottom with poles—it being so irregular and clumpy (perhaps, better, lumpy)—and to even *think* about sculling in, of course, that was more than absurd, and so the only thing which appeared at all practicable, our hero did. He took a coil of rope over his shoulder, jumped overboard with it, leaving one end fast on board, dived under the surface, so that the sea would not wash him back, paying out the rope as he advanced, and at last reached a rock under the water, took a turn with it, but this large coir rope—almost large enough to be called "hawser"—snapped like tow, and away went the canoe again at the rate of knots to leeward, before the wind, and along came Finau at a greater rate, for he caught the canoe again, jumped on board, hauled inboard the remaining part of the hawser, renewed the bailing, called out to the women to renew the masticating, and this prodigy of a man, with his steam arm and steam gullet, kept on again some fourteen hours longer, when we reached Lekeba.

And now the wind had considerably subsided, but the sea as high as ever, with a tremendous surf on the reefs, and the crew observing this latter, one of them remarked that no man could swim through it and live! when Finau observed, with some vehemence and more disdain—about the second or third time, at the utmost, that he had condescended to open his lips for the last thirty hours to a living soul— "that that remark held good only with would-be men, and not with *bona fide* ones," jumping overboard, saying, "See a real man do it!" And whilst we were going through the comparatively smooth passage with the canoe, he was going through that tremendous surf, and arrived on the beach just ahead of us, but instead of stopping there as *we* were fain to do, he still pursued his way up this somewhat steep beach, crossing it completely, got above highwater mark, "scratching gravel" with the very same motions as though still swimming in water, and would have continued to do so in defiance of all obstacles—rocks, scrub, stones, hills, and all—had not about half the inhabitants of the adjacent village plied him with heavy assuaging propitiatory offerings of property, as they thronged each side of him on a good brisk trot, in order to keep pace with him, as he continued the "gravel scratching" business, at such a tremendous rate!

I N a week or so, Finau, as the bad weather had by this time entirely subsided, proposed that they should make another effort to reach their country, when these fellows made answer that there was yet plenty of time and that they should continue to divert themselves in the usual mode of strolling about among the Fijians, or, in other words, to loaf and sponge on the latter as they had been doing for a long time past—so long, that they had long since acquired the unenviable sobriquets of "land-sharks"! But when they had completely worn their welcome out, and the following the smoke of the ovens began to be quite a stale game, and also that the doors of the houses of their hitherto entertainers began to be closed against them, and that almost in their very faces, they then came in a body to Finau, and requested that they might be allowed to make one more final effort to get his canoe up into Tonga; but this astute gentleman said that a canoe was a canoe, whether in Fiji or Tonga, and was equally useful in either country, and that he should advise that they should still continue to divert themselves by strolling about among the Fijians, say, for a couple or three years, at the very least, for instance.

Most of these fellows were years before they reached Tonga—the communication between the two countries being extremely precarious—some of them never did! But Ratu Finau betook himself down to the lee part of Fiji, where his canoe was the means of rendering him a man of importance, although it is not only quite possible but feasible also to live—and live well too—on these much-favoured islands without being owner of a large canoe, but still one is much better off with than without one.

He amassed properties in great quantities, and as he was single and far from being ill-favoured, it was not long before an attachment sprang up between himself and a Fiji maiden—they, as a general thing, having an eye to *means* as well as love—but as the whole of the inhabitants of the village in which he resided were not equally interested as direct relations of this (it is said) most eligible girl, some remark respecting his being a "luve ne yale" —stranger in a disdainful sense—by the jealous parties, and Finau getting wind of this by some means or other, of course, it was more than sufficient with a character of such very pronounced views, to knock the whole thing, girl and all, into a cocked hat, at once! After this, he lived for years wifeless, nothing daunted by the clamouring of all the male relations of the discarded, besides the incessant squabblings of perhaps a dozen other females respecting who should be the lucky possessor of this rich and brave captain and owner—but they were reckoning without their host!

At last Finau became poorly, and as he was not of the *common* mortal mould, consequently could not brook the idea of anything which pointed to lingering sickness, so he got the Fijians to haul his canoe up alongside his house, under the pretence of having an eye to it till convalescence was fully restored; but each night, whilst the Fijians were fast asleep, Ratu Finau was very active in amassing quantities of dry coco-nut leaves, and all other combustible matters, with which he filled his house, and then ignited it, and so burned all his riches, house, canoe, and his own body up in this one conflagration—raising quite a respectable funeral pile with his own hands, passing away as he had lived—the perfect hero, as he thought, poor man! and what shall we say about it? "Judge not, lest ye be judged!"

A ND now that poor Finau has been satisfactorily disposed of, satisfactorily in as far as regards myself, as he has now been in that blessed of all states—oblivion! for the last forty-four or five years —a state which I ought and should have been in long ago, if I had been plucky enough to have met it, in defiance of all that hypocritical cant which those enthusiastic scamps would cram one with, were he fool enough to swallow it—never for one moment contributing to the bodily wants, because that would touch the pocket! and which behaviour in the eyes of the savages—who, by the by, are mostly all, if not exactly generous, hospitable to a proverb, whatever their other faults—considerably retards the growth of the work they professedly came to do, and which they are so well paid for, when we take into account the luxurious kind of Nabob life many of them enjoy.

The reader, no doubt, will fully appreciate the

fact, that, if I had not the necessary pluck to com-
mit suicide, I had the more *real* pluck to live on!

And now I started again in another canoe, which,
opportunely for me, was bound for Tonga, the only
outlet for me out of Thakobau's[1] clutches, unless I
buried myself in the heart of the bush of Viti Levu
among those very petty cannibals!—a thing I never
had the most distant intention of doing—I the more
readily embraced this opportunity, as another one
might not occur for a year—perhaps two or even
three—and then it might be too late, as I might
long before that time be in the oven! Notwithstanding that I was fully awake to the risk I was continually running by delay, I never allowed that fact
to disturb my peace in the slightest, seeing there was
really no help for it, but worked on mechanically, as
it were, with the greatest *sang-froid*. As things
cropped up appearing advantageous to me, so I embraced them.

We started, this time, with nothing but males,
amounting to, perhaps, twenty-five, all told, the
greater part of them being full-grown men, the rest
lads, some five or six only—of from thirteen to sixteen years old.

[1] Or Cakobau.

CANNIBAL JACK

Things progressed in the usual way—eating, drinking, steering, sailing, and bailing, with the enlivening songs which we were all cheered by, as well as by the beating of the large wooden drum.

We had prayers morning and evening. On the third day out we sighted the two islands of Tofua and Kaau, they being the most western of the Hapai group. On one of these is an active volcano. These are the only high islands in the group. All the rest of the somewhat numerous islands are low, coral formations. It was at one of these two, and which are but a few miles apart, that the unfortunate Captain Bligh, of the *Bounty* mutiny renown, came into collision with these islanders, the latter so heartlessly stoning, and badly wounding too, some of his much distressed boat's crew, when making that exceedingly long passage in that small boat, which has long since become historical, and well it might, especially the boat episode portion of it, considering the dreadful privations endured; but these privations do not, by any means, exceed what I have myself often gone through, and which, if I live long enough and retain my faculties, I intend giving to the ungrateful world!

The natives made so sure that we should shortly

be at our destination, that they began fetching out the heads of tortoiseshell which a good few of them had in their baskets, desiring me to purchase it with cloth, which I had in one of my two chests, so as to enable them to land decently clothed among their countrymen. I had purchased several heads, and had quite satisfied the owners by allowing them to select the patterns they chose to point out. They were also well pleased with the quantity, but there was one fellow who proved to be an exceedingly cantankerous creature indeed—a thing one generally meets with and especially in those early times. He was not satisfied with the quality or quantity which I offered him. It was pretty evident that it was the first head of shell he had ever owned, and that he thought he had a little fortune! He wanted about three times its value, and was very abusive besides. I told him that there was no harm done, and that he had better keep the shell and sell it to some other foreigner, closing the chest and then put the key in my pocket, at which he flew into a violent passion, and would certainly have pushed me overboard, had it not been for the good offices of some of the more pacific ones, who prevented him.

We were within less than twenty miles of these

two islands, with a leading light breeze. We had prayers, thanking God with heartfelt gratitude for His merciful protection over this—to us—long expanse of open ocean which we had now left behind, we hoped for good, beseeching Him to continue, if not strengthen the breeze, so that we might safely as well as shortly arrive at our destination. I believe this prayer was fervent with every soul on board the canoe. We rose from our knees with full confidence that we had been heard! Grog was now prepared and which we quaffed with considerable confiding gusto, and yet the wind became lighter and lighter, till at last it subsided into only occasional puffs at intervals and from different quarters, and eventually became a dead calm, when it was decided that the sail should be lowered down and the sculling had recourse to. This was accordingly done—the natives working like horses, spelling each other when exhausted, propelling the canoe quite three miles an hour; but after about two hours of this arduous work, it began to look cloudy in the direction of the land ahead, and then puffed and lulled alternately, still looking blacker and fiercer. At last it came stronger, with no lulls, when the sculling was abandoned as useless! And to add to all our misfortunes, we now discovered that the food which had all been cooked at the last meal, and one half put away to be eaten cold at a future occasion, had all been purloined by some of the greedy portion of these rightly named "land sharks," and eaten on the sly in the hold.

And now it blew in very heavy squalls, accompanied by piercing cold rain, and, as it was now night and the sea rising rapidly, which continually washed over the whole of the canoe, at last the bailing was abandoned as useless, the two parts of the canoe being now full of water, one sea, heavier still, sweeping the decks of every conceivable thing—the cooking earth-box, my two chests, and all the natives' riches, and, in fact, everything else—and as these seas succeeded each other at very short intervals, they knocked the canoe below the surface of the water, sometimes entirely from under our feet, and, our hands being numb with cold, we could not well hold on to anything, and besides, there was very little left to hold on to, excepting the house in midships, which was still, we hoped, intact. The mast, yards, and sail were thrown overboard after incessant toil in cutting away the rigging, many of the poor natives lost in the performance! This light-

ened the canoe, apparently, but still the decks were
nearly or quite a foot under water. They attempted
to pray, but the seas filled their mouths full of salt
water so that they could not articulate a word, and
even if they had it could not have been heard by the
very next companion of misery for the roaring of
the wind and sea, etc. Some of their bodies whilst
in this position were rolled quite clear of the canoe
never to return again! I had the presence of mind
to cut clear of the yards one of the halliards before
they went away altogether, and with which I lashed
myself firmly round the middle, to the strong back
railing of the platform top of the house, where I
sat, if not quite contented, at least quite indifferent!

When daylight broke, two thirds of the crew were
missing. It was now a steady, strong, dry gale, but
no longer a hurricane, and it dried somewhat my
saturated clothes, and my teeth ceased somewhat
the incessant chattering, which had been their wont
for the last twelve hours, and especially when I had
recourse to the indispensable effort of keeping them
firmly closed together. The few natives left were
in a much worse plight than myself, by what I saw
one of them doing, as the sharks had now found us
out, and were devouring their helpless, almost dead

bodies before their very faces. I saw one poor wretch feebly contending with a shark close by him, for the entrails of one of his canoe mates which were being voraciously devoured by this monster of the deep!—hunger in his case, poor fellow, being much stronger than the inevitable danger he was now in, but in a very short time afterwards hunger and danger were both ended together!

The native who had the jangle with me respecting the price of the tortoiseshell made an effort to gain the top of the house, by making as desperate a clutch at my leg as his feeble condition would admit of, with an oath, whether to jerk me overboard, in his partial insanity, poor fellow, as perhaps he still viewed me as somewhat of an enemy, or whether to gain a safe sitting like myself, of course, I could not tell; but, either way, he failed, being too feeble, and fell backwards into the water, when the sharks, which were now in scores, nay, hundreds, made short work of him as they did of all the rest!

And yet this revolting sight did not at all shock me, or cause any fear in me. I merely looked on this horrid drama in a kind of vague, matter-of-fact, and indifferent manner—not caring two straws for anything—life, death, or even eternity! And so, of course, I did not pray, either audibly or otherwise, or even *think* about it!

IT may be asked by some, especially the cavilling portion of my readers, how it was that all the natives so easily succumbed and that in so short a time —myself alone being left? My simple answers to these simple questions are, in the first place, that they, although men, most of them, of twelve-stone weight and upwards, and from five feet nine to six feet— sometimes more—in height, and in the prime of life —strong as horses for a heavy lift or two, at the spurt of the moment, had not the stamina that a comparatively dwarfish John Bull, nearer nine than ten stone weight at his fattest, and barely five feet five inches in height when stretched to his straightest, in consequence of having lived during the whole of his youth, on good fat beef and mutton, veal, sucking pigs, and poultry of every description, cooked in the best of style; flour, milk, tea, coffee, and eggs, in a healthy part of a cold, bracing country like England, besides plenty of old home-brewed beer—frequently from six to seven years old—some good port, sherry, and other foreign wines, to say nothing of good Hollands gin and water, hot every night during the winter months—vegetables of every description, puddings, pies, tarts, jellies, custards, from four to six meals a day for sixteen years—a good appetite to eat and drink all these things as well as hundreds of other things in the shape of hot rolls and toast and muffins all smothered with beautiful fresh butter, welsh rabbits, sausages, veal cutlets, game, fish, venison, ices, creams, sillabubs, and when it came to fruits,—but then what's the good of enumerating,—I will just mention, for instance, strawberries, when in season, of the best quality as we grew them ourselves, and as for quantity something in the shape of a peck-measure full in a bucketful— or pailful as it is called—of cream! and so the power of endurance was all on my side, I think, considering this good foundation. Besides, the natives— those who were left in the morning—had gone through so much the previous eighteen or twenty hours, that they had hardly any desire to live— rather the contrary! And that is the reason that suicide is so very common on so many of the islands of the North and South Pacific Oceans, because when demoralized by panic or fear, if they do not there and then lay violent hands upon themselves, they generally pine to death—their minds being of a flabby constituency as well as their bodies!

After all this, all that I remember is, that the main part of the canoe—the big one of the two—parted from the decking completely, and drifted clear away, but the decks still held together, but were reduced to an angle of about thirty degrees of inclination, in consequence of the other and smaller canoe being still intact, causing my body to droop forward in its fast, strong rope-lashings, so that I was now suspended by the middle, still, however, retaining my seat, somewhat after the fashion of a public-house sign, which I had in my youth frequently seen in London, and called the "Golden Fleece."

How long I remained in this position—whether a week, a day, an hour or two, or even a month—if possible for the human body to retain its vital spark for this last conjectured long period—it is impossible for me to say, as I had no means of ascertaining, even approximately, because I did not know even the name of the month, to say nothing of its date, when that little amusing episode took place. All that I know is, that *sometime* after this, in my incipient state of regaining consciousness, I just unclosed my eyes for about two seconds—no more—

and was then fain to close them again from languid weakness; but still they were unclosed long enough for me to get a glimpse that I was not alone, but in the company of an angel, I thought—not a white one, but a black one—and that there was something superlatively pleasant as well as wonderfully mysterious about it, because it is said that they "neither marry nor are given in marriage" in the angelic regions, which, of course, implies that they are of the neuter gender, whereas this one was of the feminine gender! It was like a vision of a heavenly aspect, and so I lay, at least, twelve days longer, before I thoroughly recovered full consciousness, and which I did, however, by degrees, at the expiration of that long period; but should I live for a thousand years longer, I shall never forget the soothing, placid happiness which I experienced the whole of that twelve days, whilst hovering between the two worlds! To make a long story short, I was in the bush on a Fiji island, under a large banyan tree, with a Fiji girl watching me; but before I regained full consciousness I felt that I was in heaven—and if heaven proves to be half as blissful a state as those days were to me, then it is, indeed, worth trying to gain at whatever sacrifice!

CANNIBAL JACK

I felt that I was in my mother's company, and who, by the by, died a thorough saint, albeit I had never known her in this grosser world, but I did there in that heavenly one, also my sister, Marianne, who also died a most exemplary Christian. I was given to understand that I was there partly through their prayers—the latter reminding me of that solemn warning she had given me ten minutes previous to her death, when she called me closer to her dying bed, and repeated my Christian name three distinct times—"William, William, William, *Remember your dying sister!*"

I thought that we were all mixed in one rapturous joy, in the company of innumerable angels—black and white. The Virgin Mary, also her blessed Son, were there also, and they were all receiving me with unfeigned delight!

When I found that I was really and truly back to this sublunary state, I felt, for the moment, horribly disappointed!

This girl, when I opened my eyes for the first time for those few seconds only, and whom I took to be an angel, and which appeared to me to be enacted in another world, or a mere vision only, and not at all a reality, was then plying me with sustenance, consisting of the nice, white, delicate, soft, custard-like meat, mixed with the heated milk or water of the delicious young coco-nuts, by gently parting my lips with her tender fingers for the reception of the same, and which act, together with its reviving influence, no doubt caused me to partially (but exceedingly evanescently) recover; but, as I said above, I immediately afterwards relapsed into that languid weakness, and continued in that state, she said, for twelve consecutive days,—she continuing all that long period to ply me with that and other nutritious sops at regular stated intervals, day and night, without for one moment relaxing this exceedingly kind and more than human vigilance, excepting for the purpose of rest, and now and then returning to the village for the sake of allaying suspicion, should her absence become too prolonged, and thereby become suspicious.

She told me that during all that time I occasionally opened my eyes as at first, merely looking at her, and then closed them again as before; but during the last four or five days of this "long sleep," as she called it, this opening of the eyes happened oftener and continued longer, till, at last, I recovered entirely, that is, in regard to consciousness and strength too.

"I looked about me," she said, "with apparent great wonderment," and at last answered all her incessant questionings.

She now told me that I was on the small island of "Komo" in the "lau" or windward group of Fiji, subject to Lekeba, the residence of Tuniau, the king, "and that she herself was the daughter of the chief of this island, residing in the only village or township on the island, and that it was situated just round the point"—the distance being about a mile off, I afterwards learned—"and that, whilst searching for shell-fish along the shore at a distance from the village, and quite out of sight of it, she had been the first to discover the small part of a large sailing canoe, stranded on the shingly beach hard by, with myself lashed so securely to the back rail or banister of the canoe house, and that she had great difficulty in getting me clear when she first essayed to cast off the rope with her fingers; but perceiving my large, and, as it proved to be sharp knife, she quickly drew it from its sheath and severed the different parts of the rope, and then conveyed me on her back up to the spot where we were now sitting upon for inter-

ment, as she thought I was dead, and that she would
not take me to the village, even had she been able,
because the people there were not like herself 'lotu'
(religious) and would be sure to cut up some capers
with my body, and even perhaps eat it, when they
found that it did not yet stink, and that all her en-
treaties would be of no avail, because she was not
like one of Tuniau's daughters of Lekeba, he being
a great king, whereas her father was only a chief of
a small island, consequently the people cared very
little about him, and, of course, much less for herself
—she being a mere girl! But as she had learned to
read in God's book, whilst at Mrs. Calvert's school
at Lekeba, where her father had left her when he
went in to pay his yearly tribute to Tuniau, and that
book had told her to be good to everybody, and more
especially to the unfortunate and afflicted, and when
she found I was alive and not dead as she at first
thought, she had constantly prayed to God for my
perfect recovery, and that He had answered her
prayers by making me well again!"

And now I asked her how it would be with me
if I ventured into the village in her company,
whether her father would receive me and not kill
me? She said that *he* himself would not hurt me for

her sake, she being his only daughter, and that her mother was dead. I then said, but perhaps the people will insist upon "knocking the salt water from my eyes"—as it is termed—fearing the god of the sea more than your father? She said that she would have to consider this well over, asking God's help, before she could venture to give me an answer to this most difficult question: "taro dredre."

I now inquired for my knife and also for my belt, which she produced from a hollow of a rotten knot of the tree, where she had deposited them for safe keeping. I found the 100 sovereigns quite correct, which it will be remembered by the reader that I had received as a reward for my perseverance, when I acted in the capacity of detective in recovering the whole of the missing 1,000*l.* which had been purloined from the "Sailor Boy"—the pugilistic hero—by a native. She said she had discovered this inner belt when she stripped me for the purpose of rinsing my clothes as well as my body with fresh water, so as to cleanse them of the remains of the salt water. The part of this remark which alluded particularly to the rinsing of my body, although it is generally thought that dark people's blushes are never visible, but that is a wrong conclusion, because this most delicate as well as religious girl, more than I ever witnessed before with either black or white, blushed so palpably, and, more than that, could never afterwards be induced by any means to make the most distant allusion to that particular part of the subject, but always so adroitly turned the conversation on to some other subject!

One day, on her regular return to me, from her father's at the village, which she never omitted to visit, on the pretence of carrying home a basket of shell-fish, for the very requisite purpose of throwing dust into the eyes of all the rest of these very acute savages as well as his own, and thereby to account for her frequent and sometimes longish absences, in order to secure ample time for her self-imposed work of mercy, in regard to seeing to the well-being of her now convalescent protégé.

And now, I suspect, if to judge by my own feelings, she viewed me in the shape of her truly affianced partner, sent to her by the hand and will of that all-providing Providence, and in whom she so implicitly believed and so fully trusted, in her simple but strong faith. I say, on this particular day she seemed unusually sad, when I, of course, wished to know, at any rate, *something* of its cause; but the

138

only answer I got, and that after long waiting for, from this more than woman in regard to sentiment, was a most ungovernable burst of grief and uncontrollable torrent of tears and sobs, ejaculating and bemoaning her hard fate, declaring in a most heart-rending paroxysm of grief that she was utterly undone—"*Au saca!*" "*Au saca sara!!*"

After this violent grief (this violent paroxysm almost annihilating her) had somewhat subsided, and something like reason began to assume its wonted sway, I managed to elicit—piecemeal as it were—from her, that the people of the town had been collecting property, preparatory to presenting it to her father, according to the immemorial heathen custom, so as to celebrate the shortly forthcoming marriage between herself and the lad to whom she had been ceremoniously betrothed in her infancy, and this first ceremony had been confirmed by stated periodical instalments of property-gifts ever since, up till now that she had arrived at the full age of puberty, between sixteen and seventeen —the girls of the tropics being precocious in body as well as mind. And now the dreaded climax was at hand!

I asked her "if she did not like the lad?" When

this hitherto more than lamb in gentleness, turned, for the nonce, more than tigress, in the vehemence of the two passions which had, for the time being, taken complete possession of her, said, "I liked him well enough till I saw you, you little, blind, white fool! but not in the way I like you, and I insist upon you liking me in the same manner!" when she clasped me with such a passionate embrace, that I really thought that she would squeeze the very life out of me! and then as suddenly desisted, forcing me on to my knees, herself assuming the same posture, and poured out her whole soul in the most eloquent supplications, asking forgiveness for her waywardness, and help and strength from above to guide her in the right path for the future!

She got up, now transformed into an angel of light and meekness!

This girl's form was of that sylph-like symmetry so common to the nymphs of the South Sea Islands, and especially at that time—before degeneracy had begun to set in—and her features of such exquisite regularity, while her eyes were liquid with love and adoration! Her skin, though dark, not black, was as soft, smooth, and glossy as the most beautiful of silk-velvet, and the long tapering fingers of her beautiful aristocratic hands, capable of being bent as far backwards, almost, as they were forwards, in their exceeding pliability, besides the beauty of her neatly turned ankles and her exquisitely formed feet. Her teeth were perfectly regular and as white as snow, and the *tout ensemble* of this lovely creature, and which I do not know what to compare it to, unless perhaps the human gazelle, fairly ravished me, and her name was "Ande Litia"—Miss Litia!

About this time a trading schooner from the second biggest island of Fiji—Vanua Levu—and from the district called Soleau situated on that large island, and which the whites, since their expulsion from Levuka by Cakobau, had made their permanent residence, came along on a trading expedition, and when night came on soon after her arrival, this girl put into the water with her own hands, unperceived by a single soul but herself, a small paddling canoe, and paddled it up to the shingly beach, and hastened up to the banyan tree, and forthwith proceeded to hurry me down to the canoe, and then paddled me off to the schooner, saying that God had answered her many prayers, and that she now saw her way clear of all danger of the salt-water being knocked out of my eyes, and securing me for her own and only husband, besides; because she would put me on board the schooner that night and the next day I could land with her in the regular way, as she would carry on board some presents in the shape of a fowl or two, some fruit, etc., the next morning, and select me for her friend—a thing always allowed even in the wildest times; and then I could land as one of the crew, and go up in the ordinary way to her father's house with her as his daughter's friend, without being in the slightest danger from the people of the village, "magaiti-nada!" —a curse, which will not here bear a literal interpretation, especially as it comes from the pretty lips of the religious and moral Litia herself! Suffice it to say, that it has reference to their mothers, and is, after all, only a little harmless expletive, used by this sorely tried poor girl in her excitement. When we were within hearing distance and almost or quite within sight, it not being very dark, I hailed the schooner in English, and as the man who had anchor watch could perceive at a glance, as it were, that no treachery was intended, he allowed me to come on board, and this brave girl paddled me up alongside, not really sure that she would not be fired at, it being night, as the whole of the whites at Fiji, at that time, most religiously guarded against all communication with the natives during the hours of darkness—and which fact most of the natives were aware of—whilst on a trading expedition, lest treachery might supervene—a thing they were shockingly prone to throughout the whole length and breadth of this proverbially treacherous country!

I now told her to hasten back to the shore, haul the canoe up in its place, go to bed, and come on board with her presents the next morning, as arranged—myself remaining on board the schooner.

The next morning, bright and early, she was on board with her fowls, fruit, a couple of fancy mats, etc., her little brother paddling the canoe this time for her. She jumped on board, when I immediately made up to her, bidding her good morning ("Sai-adra!"), as though I had never seen her before, asking her in the purest Fiji if she had come to trade these things off for property, or if she preferred forming a connection in the shape of friendship, which in Fiji is called "veitau"? This completely blinded the brother—a lad of some twelve years old —as to our former acquaintance. She made answer that she would prefer making the things a present to

143

myself, seeing that I was so very fluent in her own language, she said.

No. 17

I ACCORDINGLY accepted this present, took a couple of sovereigns from my belt, retired into the cabin, expended it principally in print, together with other accessories—such as needles, cotton, thimble, tape, buttons, etc., etc., in fact, all and sundry which go to the making up a lady's toilet, and which, by the by, is no very great deal when the recipient is a *Fiji* lady. I also bought a large fourteen-inch knife for her father, when we betook ourselves to the canoe, the boy paddling for the shore as highly rejoiced as if his sister had suddenly come into a large fortune—and it was a fortune to her, poor girl!

We landed, and as I passed up towards the chief's house, the girl leading the way, I saw under a shed —a mere sun-break—the part of the canoe which had been my salvation, and so very nearly, alas! my destruction too.

As I looked at it, the girl gave me a very significant glance, which meant, as plainly as words could have said, "There's your old friend!" It was now converted into a very nice single canoe, called a "cama kau," and which name conveys its own meaning—a canoe with a single, wooden spar outrigger. It was even now capable of carrying quite a score of people, with perfect safety, in ordinary weather. I saw also a largish sail, spread out on the nice little grass plot beside the shed, very near completion, made from the new, narrow, sail-matting. She also gave me another significant look, confirming what I was then thinking, that this latter was for my "old friend."

We entered her father's house without molestation, and, in fact, excepting for their notorious cannibalism—and which horrid practice, by the by, they have inherited from their forefathers—these simple people, and especially those of almost all the small islands, one would take, on his first entrance among them, to be quite civilized, so civil, orderly, and domestic, apparently, are all their almost patriarchal bearings, and their countenances wear a contented and even benevolent expression; and were it not for the rites of their horrid, false, and heathen religion, they would be all they ordinarily appeared. As it is, they but seldom have an opportunity of exercising these horrid rites, unless some foolish unfortunates like myself happen to drop into their clutches, sent by the sea god, and they always drop into their capacious maws, unless thwarted by the wily stratagems of such prodigies as Litia, as in my own, so far, lucky case!

Litia presented her father with the long knife, and which would prove an exceedingly useful article to him for numberless purposes—such as clearing away bush when cutting new gardens, or weeding old ones; cutting off the branches of bananas from the trees of the dozen—more or less—different species, when mature, ready for hanging up to ripen, this plan being generally adopted, instead of the more natural one of being left to become so on the trees, because the birds in this country are especially troublesome—parrots principally—and there the flying-fox or vampire bat—whether bird or beast or a little of both—can go his share of ripe bananas as well as all other kinds of fruit. And then the knife is exceedingly useful for cutting the tree itself down, and cutting it into pieces to scatter over the ground to become manure, instead of uselessly encumbering the earth after it has borne the one and only bunch it ever bears, and giving its suckers a chance of sun, light, and air, so as to enable them to bear in their turn the same as their mothers.

She told him that she had secured this useful article especially for himself, from her good "friend," pointing to me, asking in a very playful manner, if she was not an excellent judge of human nature in respect to generosity, in the selection of her friend? She also exhibited all her own riches, prattling away all the time with the greatest glee, and then tore off from her print three or four fathoms, and straightway proceeded to equip her brother in the accustomed style which they use the native tappa or "masi" for, and he being a chief's son it formed a train which commoner youths dare not adopt, and with which he aired his consequence, by immediately dragging it all through the dirt, throughout the whole village, as pleased as a dog with two tails!

They then proceeded to make a small feast for me, as it was through my means that he had been first breeched, and consequently—rather prematurely— made a man of, his hitherto state being perfectly nude, whereas it was now only partially so, and as this metamorphosis is always accompanied by a rejoicing ceremonial feast, exchanging of gifts, a dance, etc., etc., and so, not two, but in this case, three birds were killed by the one stone—to wit, the making me welcome, and actually adopting me, as it were, into this very interesting family, besides consecrating this, always considered momentous change.

The whole of the simple inhabitants of this village were rendered extremely happy at the celebration of this little episode, and the father of Litia was at the height of his glory at having his boy turned into a man so suddenly, and all through the good offices of his more than idolized daughter; and seeing that he was a widower of not more than forty years of age, the whole of his hitherto concentrated conjugal affections had been transferred to this living type of his never to be forgotten, but for ever lost, faithful partner! Seeing that these small isolated places are so monotonously cut off from all the rest of the outside world, no wonder that the least excitement out of the ordinary humdrum routine tends to elate these poor people to a degree scarcely credible—in fact, it is something comparable to being brought from *death* itself to *life* itself!

They were so prodigiously rejoiced that they were never tired of telling me "that whenever I called again—and which they sincerely hoped would be often—that I knew where to make straight for my real home"!

But it soon began to appear that this kind of merely tacit adoption, which seemed to satisfy everybody else, would not by any means satisfy Litia, whose expectations were decidedly of a more tangible form, and me being adopted into the family so that I should always have a home whenever I occasionally called—if ever, by the by!—on my return trips, as these simple blockheads thought, would not, of course, suit this self-willed beauty. She knew her power and acted accordingly. She aimed at nothing short of adoption, and absorption too, of my whole being, body and soul, into her very essence! No half-measures for Litia! for when the time came for me to repair on board the schooner for the purpose of proceeding on to Lekeba, and at the arrival of the boat on the beach to convey me on board, the hand-shaking business was prolonged with that lingering procrastination, easier imagined, under the circumstances, than described! but when it came that I *must* go or be left for good, in essaying to embark, I was held on to with that desperate tenaciousness, and even franticness, which is almost impossible to describe!

CANNIBAL JACK

The whole of the people of the village were down at the beach, and they tried to console her by saying that, as soon as the vessel had gone, the ceremony of marriage with her betrothed would be performed, and that it had only been postponed for a more leisurely time, as all the property had some time previously been collected in readiness to convey to her father, and his brother, her uncle, called in Fiji little father—"tamana lailai"; but instead of consoling, this irritated her to the last degree, and when her affianced, at the suggestion of all the bystanders, offered to lead her away, she spurned and spit at him, declaring, that even if she loved him instead of hating him as she implacably did, she said, she wished to know how or by whose means this ceremony could be performed?—marrying a heathen to a Christian, most absurd and preposterous! she said. And now her uncle attempted to drag her forcibly away, but in dragging her he was dragging me also, for it was next to impossible to unclasp her hands from around my body, which she had so firmly clasped in her almost frantic despair, as well as her determination to carry her point! She declared that she would strangle herself (a thing there was not much doubt about, as they were always terribly prone to suicide) unless she was allowed to have the husband, whom God in His goodness had sent to her, in answer to her many prayers!

And now the father stepped up to me and whispered in my ear, that although it was not for him, an ignorant black man, to dictate to a white gentleman from the wise land ("vanna vuka"), yet he thought as she had in the first place saved my life the least I could do was now to save hers! And so it appeared that this real good fellow was in the secret as well as his daughter how I had first arrived on the island; this intelligence, of course, had been communicated to him by his loving and confiding offspring.

The boat's crew, thinking that this girl was and had been, some time previous to this, my *bona fide* wife, as they knew next to nothing of my previous history, and that she was merely objecting, albeit with extreme vehemence, to me going to Lekeba, got tired of this somewhat prolonged and not very amusing drama, shoved off, when her father said aloud to me, "Take her into Lekeba and get married by Mr. Calvert," but I remarked "that if that was his real intention I could find a much handier shop than Lekeba to accomplish that little matter," when he said that that was, of course, his real intention, because he had not the slightest desire to run the risk of losing his daughter by strangulation, or even for her to live unhappy. As all the people looked greatly surprised, if not exactly shocked, at this declaration, I asked, "What about the betrothed lad?" and this young man hearing me, said, *"Au sa cata, Au sa cata vakadua sara!"* which was equivalent to forswearing this very perverse affianced of his for ever! I then hailed the boat again, when she returned and took us both on board—she being nothing loth—and we repaired to the schooner, where I bought an assortment of goods, among the rest ten muskets, a pig of lead, and a keg of powder, besides several large boxes of military percussion caps, ball moulds, etc., expending some twenty-five or thirty sovereigns from my belt. We were both put on shore again with the goods, when the boat returned to the schooner, and she was immediately got under way, set sail, and proceeded on her voyage, and that was the last I ever saw of her. The things were all carried to the chief's house, where all three of us followed, and then I sent over to the betrothed lad a quantity of stuff—a new American axe, a couple of tomahawks, some knives, etc.,—and which would greatly assist him in procuring another wife. The chief's brother received also an American axe, which I had sent across the way for him, and I did all this for the sake of keeping peace and quietness, and prevent all dissatisfaction, consequently all chance of an irruption would thereby be avoided as far as it was possible for human foresight to guard against.

I NOW proposed that the large single sailing canoe —my "old friend!"—should be put in the water, and that the virgin trip, under her new form, should be gone through with on the morrow, as the wind was quite favourable, that is, that it was leading both to and from Ogea, the island we were bound to.

We arrived safe and sound at this my old habitat, the canoe behaving remarkably well, where I, with some little difficulty, aided with a nice little douceur in the shape of about three fathoms of double-width white shirting—a thing much sought after, especially by the teachers, catechists, etc.—prevailed upon the ordained native pastor, an old acquaintance of mine, to forgo the usual ceremony of publishing the banns three separate Sundays consecutively, and substitute a weekday, and one day only, for the calling our names aloud in the church, or *chapel*, I believe is the approved term for the Wesleyans, and then marry us directly afterwards on the same day,—something in the shape of Paddy the sentry, when he said, "Who goes there three time?" bang!! This was accordingly done, and as Litia's father was the only one there to give her away, he was obliged to put a piece of calico round his middle before he could enter the chapel, and as this "covering the person" is considered throughout the South Sea Islands a preliminary to embracing the Christian faith, and whenever the question of "Does he or she—as the case may be—wear cloth?" it is always understood as being synonymous with the question "Is he or she—as the case may be—religious?"

After that this little business was completely concluded, quite to the satisfaction of all parties concerned, and more especially the most interested personages—Litia and myself—we twain having been in so extemporized a manner metamorphosed into one flesh, according to the rites and ceremonies of "Holy Mother Church," which appellation, I suppose, they are as much entitled to as their prototypes,

CANNIBAL JACK

Roman Catholics and Church of England, they—the Wesleyans—having conducted themselves with great propriety for a matter of a couple of centuries, consequently with very extensive usefulness, we repaired back again to Komo, taking the pastor's younger brother with us to form a new church on this our own island, the chief having renounced all idolatry from the first moment that he had put the cloth on at the giving away his daughter.

The next day after our arrival at home, the young catechist commenced, *pro tem.*, his pastoral duties in the chief's house, till a permanent chapel should be erected—consisting of divine service, school, and tentative lessons, all of which were performed with great regularity and decorum by this very energetic young man, he having brought over with him from his brother at Ogea a quantity of tracts containing Scripture portions, slates, pencils, etc., all of which I had purchased from that ordained native, and so, an embryo chapel was set going on this hitherto heathen island—the whole of the congregation, at present, consisting of no more than Litia, her father, myself, and the chief's young and only son, Litia's brother, and, of course, my brother-in-law.

This all went on very well, apparently, for some

time, the people, some of them, coming along for the purpose of witnessing the new ceremony, hearing the singing of the religious hymns, sometimes joining in it themselves as they stood looking on, with something akin to interest, just outside the "big house," and, at last, it was proposed to me by the chief that we should organize a "so levu" (kind of fair) and clothe all the people in order to draw them into the new religion, I standing almost the whole brunt of the expense, and I even paid for some of the pigs, fowls, etc., which were slaughtered for their consumption upon this occasion—eating and drinking being the principal items in this as well as most all other performances of savages! They all participated in the advantages of this "so levu," and, for the time being, clothed themselves, some of them with mine and Litia's print, the rest with the chief's "tappa," but all in the religious style, about a moiety of the whole remaining true to the last, after some considerable vacillation, in their new profession, but the remaining portion again relapsed into their old heathenism—the chief's brother alone refusing from the first to have aught to do with it, saying in a very indignant tone, "that it was a likely thing, indeed, that he should condescend to be clothed in a petticoat ("liku") and be made a woman of, and all for the sake of obliging a friendless child"—myself, and here called "luvenigale"— "who ought to have had the salt water knocked from his eyes in the first place"—the mode of my landing having, long since, become public—"and thereby avoiding the displeasure of their own and forefather's *true* gods, and that he fully expected some dire calamity to shortly befall the whole of the place or its inhabitants!"

At any rate, the new chapel was begun, continued, and completed, without a very pronounced demonstration on the part of the antagonistic party —the chief's brother at their head—a thing I was particularly anxious to avoid, by strenuously opposing the somewhat vehement proposition of the new religious party—and who were, by the by, in the majority somewhat. The proposition was, that the heathen temple should be demolished and the chapel built on its site; but this was finally overruled and the temple allowed to remain intact, the chapel being erected on a vacant space of new ground.

Things went on, at first, very well, each party adhering to its own belief, and I began to think that the heathen would eventually be drawn over to our side, fully hoping and believing, too, that it was only a question of time; but in the meantime it began to assume a nasty, if not threatening aspect!

The little hollowed-out pieces of wood, used as drums—a substitute for bells—whenever beat for the purpose of collecting the people for the performance of divine service, school, prayers, etc., was now incessantly disturbed, and quite drowned by the clamour of the large drums of the heathen temple, and which these savages purposely beat to annoy and aggravate the religious party! All this and much more was endured with great patience and praiseworthy forbearance, but the cannibal party at last went so far as to pollute the inside of the chapel, and before the daily religious functions could be discharged, these much harassed people were obliged to clean out the filth which had been deposited overnight, and every night, the first thing every morning, besides the trouble they were put to in having to wash and dry the mats every day, necessitating them to sit on the dirty earthen floor, whilst the sun —if happily shining—was drying the latter!

Even their gardens or plantations in the bush were stolen from, and the residue wantonly cut up and destroyed, reducing the owners to very short commons. These and other atrocious acts went on for weeks, till they concluded, no doubt, that they could go any length with impunity, for one night we were all aroused from a profound sleep—the religious party being considerably fatigued by the large fishing match they had been the previous day engaged in for the want of food! The chapel was in flames, and now we all endeavoured to extinguish them, the heathen party laughing us to scorn, taunting us by saying the best thing to be done was to call down Jehova and see what He could do in the matter!

The chapel was consumed and burned completely up, notwithstanding the extraordinary efforts the religious party made till daylight to extinguish it, the heathen, armed to the teeth, rather hindering than contributing to put it out. The chief wished to know "who they were armed against? and said, I know you people set fire to the chapel!" They said, of course, we did, and the reason we are armed is that we intend to knock salt-water from the "friendless child's" eyes, which ought to have been done long ago, and if we had done it just now it would have done to extinguish the flames!

HEARING all this as well as their brutish coarse jokes and diabolical defiant laugh, I thought it was about time for me to retire, and which I did to the chief's house, where all the muskets were. I immediately proceeded to load them all with ball-cartridge, which I had had the precaution to make some time previous, to be in readiness for any emergency. I had just finished capping them all with the large military caps, and depositing them on the mats full cocked with their muzzles pointing in the direction of the open space of the doorways—the reed doors being down—and was now filling the cartridge boxes full of new cartridges, buckling one around my middle, the squabble getting more and more threatening outside every moment, when Litia came along in a terrible fright, telling me to come along with her at once, and she would show me a safe hiding-place in the bush, because her uncle would be sure to kill me, and that shortly! And whilst we were arguing the pro and con of this disagreeable business, sure enough, they all came along with Litia's uncle at their head; but the chief had got ahead of them and stood in the doorway, and tried to keep his brother from entering by bodily force and dissuasion, he having no arms in his hands, not thinking it necessary, perhaps, and besides, he did not wish to fight as long as it could be avoided, on account of the new religion he had embraced; but his brother, impatient of all obstruction, knocked him down with the back of his tomahawk and stunned him, and there he lay. He then rushed over the chief's prostrate body, shifting his spear from his left to his right hand, and the tomahawk to his left hand, not caring about facing me at too close quarters, as he saw that I had a musket in my hand and my finger on the trigger, it being full cocked. He poised the spear and quivered it at me, Litia sheltering my body all the time with her own, begging at the same time in the most suppliant accents for my life; but he cursed her with one of the worst oaths in Fiji, making a most indelicate allusion to her mother, and she being dead, and long since in her grave, even according to their own notions, rendered it worse, swearing if she did not get out of the way that he would pass the spear through the pair of us. I hesitated no longer, but pulled the trigger and shot him dead!

His followers winced for the moment at this, and which I acknowledge before the whole world that I took advantage of, by picking up the loaded muskets at my feet and discharged them right in among them, one after the other, as quick as lightning—they being already cocked—one ball in some cases passing through two or three of the bodies of these would-be murderers!

The remainder of them retreated to their spirit-temple. And now the chief recovered, and was soon sensible that his brother was dead, because Litia was now, very audibly—in fact it was howling—as well as visibly crying over this wretch's body!

He said, that since his brother was dead—albeit his own fault—that all the rest of the heathen should be killed, and forthwith proceeded towards the temple with a lighted firestick in his hand, and blew it into a blaze, igniting the temple; and as soon as they began to roast inside they rushed for the one low, narrow doorway, where they were most of them tomahawked, and the few who managed to get outside were shot down by the muskets which our people had reloaded. Some two or three were either smothered by the smoke or burned to death, as was evident by the calcined remains of their bodies after it was all over! One fellow, it was rumoured, had escaped into the bush; but as he never afterwards made his appearance, I suppose it was a false statement.

Their wives and children were given to understand that they were only saved by the merciful dictates of the gospel of forbearance, and their nominally, at any rate, embracing the Christian tenets. This they seemed very grateful to accept; but whilst all the rest of the people were very busy in preparing for the interment of the slain, the women managed to retire, unperceived, a little way back in the bush, and the first intimation of their absence was divulged by a tremendous hubbub which the children were kicking up, one of whom had gone in search of her mother, and found her to be one of a number of corpses which composed a considerable heap. The people now repaired to this revolting scene of immolation, where they found some score—more or less —of these widows all strangled with the native "tappa," which they had taken with them for the purpose of effecting the voluntary sacrifices to the manes of their unfortunate husbands; the two last of these victims, who, no doubt, had acted executioners to the rest, and at their request, were found suspended by their necks to the branch of a low tree.

CANNIBAL JACK

It appeared that these last two, after they had obliged all the rest by strangulation with the tappa or "masi"—one hauling on one side and the other on the opposite side of each victim, as they voluntarily stepped forward in their turn, till life was extinct, and then made a strong vine fast to each of their own necks, and then climbed this lowish tree, and firmly tied the opposite ends of the two respective vines to the strongest branch; and then, according to the account of the daughter of one of them—a girl of about seven years old—just as she made her appearance, attracted by the screaming lamentations of the first girl on the spot, over the corpse of *her* mother, these two woman jumped simultaneously at a given signal which they had preconcerted, and these two girls were powerless to render any assistance—even had they been old enough to have thought of such a thing, and especially in their great bewilderment—by casting off the vines, or cutting them down, had there even been a knife at hand, and besides, that would have been perfectly useless, as both the women's necks were broken! And now came the horrid, heartrending, indescribable, melancholy spectacle, as these children rolled over and over, clung and held on to, with

164

the most intolerable and inconsolable despair, the corpses of their immolated mothers! Their husbands' graves were reopened and their wives buried with them. The children had to be forcibly dragged out of the graves, whilst they were clamouring to be buried in alive with their—for ever lost to them —parents!

THIS horrid drama cast a most horrid and melancholy shade over the whole place, and it remained in that state for a very lengthened period, the whole of the people merely crawling along with no appearance of anything worthy the name of life; and as for their necessary, ordinary, simple duties, they were almost entirely neglected! They were dejected to the last degree, both in a mental and bodily point of view; and well they might, for all, or nearly all, of the departed ones were more or less related by consanguinity to these surviving ones!

The real tangible as well as beneficial effect it seemed to have was a greater clinging to the new religion, and which was the only thing they seemed to take the slightest interest in.

I felt this perhaps more acutely than anyone else,

and to add to my despondency, Litia, who was now pregnant, sickened, and all the attention, care, and embrocation, outwardly, to the affected part—the stomach—and inward herb-medicines, which these people so thoroughly understand, besides the various fomentations, good diet, composed of nourishing soups of different descriptions,—I say all these things proved of no avail, for poor Litia died, and I tried to die too, but could not, and so I was obliged to endure a living death, or more properly speaking, a death-like life, and which was, by the by, ten times worse, I suppose, than death itself!

As time wore on—that being the universal panacea for all human, mental ailments—these poor people having truly gone through the "fiery ordeal," and being led by that truly exemplary young catechist, Paula, and who was sometime previous to this proclaimed a full teacher, and at their request was allowed to continue and officiate as their regularly appointed and confirmed pastor, they began to imbibe that true consolation which nothing but penitence, added to their simple but true faith, could give, and in a very short time became proverbially a most moral and consistent people.

I managed with infinite trouble to construct a nice

headstone from a large coral slab, and carved the day and date—which I had got from Paula—of the death of my poor Litia—a girl I thought more of than all the dozens—nay, scores—of female companions I ever had before or since!

IT must not be supposed by this seemingly, perhaps, *boasting* language of mine, that I am at all glorying in a disreputable system of prostitution— nothing of the kind—I merely relate, as I am writing my life, everything which happened to me, even, at the first blush of the thing, to my own disparagement! As I was thrown, in the first place, by untoward circumstances, wholly unsought for by myself, into these outlandish countries, and being considerably disgusted at the usage I had frequently received at the hands of my own colour, and who, by the by, pretend to be at the top of the tree, in respect to humanity, fair play, etc., etc., and perceiving, without being gifted with any great amount of penetration, that it was all a farce, a boast, and a lie, I naturally concluded that it was a duty I owed to myself, to make the best of a bad bargain, and especially as I had been sent into this world, if not exactly against my will, at any rate without having a vote on the subject, to get through it as easy as practicable, and so I adopted the customs of my *pro tem.* adopted countries, on the principle of "When in Rome, to do as Romans do"! and so I took to myself a number of wives—a man being estimated by the number of the inmates of his harem, and the more wives the more property, and also the more servants, consequently the more attendance, in the same way as in so-called civilization, the more money the bigger the man!

I may possibly be asked, "What about bringing a number of creatures into the world?" I also ask, as an offset to this, what about the injunction, "Be fruitful and multiply and replenish the earth"? And then again I may be asked, "What about their souls?" As an offset to this second question, I say, those who never heard of a law ought not to be responsible to the law, excepting that law which is the father of all laws, innate to all God's creatures—the savage as well as the civilized man, and I maintain, this, even in opposition to such men as Locke himself! and others.

CANNIBAL JACK

A s it was very little use to me, remaining on Komo, bemoaning my hard fate; besides, I was far from being sure that my whereabouts was not by this time publicly known all over the Lekeba principality; and the reason I had not long since been disturbed by Cakobau's myrmidons was, no doubt, that I could be picked up at any moment that these black rascals had occasion for a white "bakola" as an "offering"—that always being the ostensible cause —whereas a good blow-out of human flesh was always the real object! By remaining on Komo I ran a double risk, because if ever sent for by the "Vasu Levu" to Lekeba, Mara, Cakobau's half-brother, I should have been immediately given up, cooked or raw, whichever way preferred, as that small island was much too insignificant, politically, to have for a moment thought of refusing any orders from Lekeba, to say nothing of the much feared, even at that early time, and all powerful Bau! And so I at once decided to proceed into the former of these two places, where Uluqalala was then living, and, although a foreigner, he was too much respected by the Fijians for them to offer to take me forcibly out of this somewhat formidable Tonga chief's residence; but if I exposed myself too carelessly in the

CANNIBAL JACK

night, outside, of course, that would be a different matter, owing to my imprudence, and I might fully expect the consequences!

When I arrived at Lekeba I went straight to Uluqalala—take notice that the letter or alphabetical character "q" is always sounded as ga, it being a missionary invention—who received me with open arms and open heart too, as he would have done had there been a score instead of one, and all, not because he was a chief or even a Christian, but because he was a *man!* When I say "not because he was a Christian," I mean I was hardly ever so received by the so-called *white* Christians,—quite the contrary,—because they, as a general thing, would allow one to perish, first considering the profit and loss of the matter!

I cruised about with this Tongan chief, all over the dependent Lekeba islands, as well as all the "Eastern Group." He travelled in state in his very large double canoe, having as many as a hundred of his subjects constantly with him—men, women, and children, as well as a large sprinkling of grown-up girls. Of the latter I need not dilate on their physical beauty, as that fact is so well known in history that the symmetry of figure, when young, and regularity of feature, as well as exceedingly good

170

expression, in most cases, have long since become proverbial in regard to the young girls of the Friendly Islands!

As we brought up each day at a separate island, there was always a feast prepared for us by the inhabitants. He was always conveyed from the canoe to the shore on a litter or hand-barrow constructed for the purpose, lest he should wet his feet—no foolish load for the bearers, over sharp coral-rocks in many places—when I state that he weighed quite twenty stone! I used to carry in the canoe a trade-chest, filled with all manner of useful articles as well as various knick-knacks, which I had purchased from a trading schooner, and with which I, in three or four weeks, purchased quite as many hundred-weight of good tortoiseshell, besides great quantities of curiosities. I was continually feasted on the very best of food by this more than good chief, and all that he ever required of me was that I should shave him, because he always declared that that process performed by me always put him to sleep, whereas when performed by any other person it always had the very opposite effect, he said; and well it might, considering the horrid scraping he had to endure, as not a soul of the whole of the natives of the two countries—Friendly Islands and Fiji—at that time knew how to set or sharpen a razor; and had he not been a professor of Christianity, I don't know how many would have bitten the dust! because it was strictly tabooed in heathen times to draw the most infinitesimal portion of a chief's blood, and allowance was never made for accidents!

At all the islands, in the parts where the chief or leading man lived, there were always buildings for the reception of visitors, generally away from the villages, removed as much as half a mile in some cases up or down the beach above high-water mark, situated on nice green plots, sheltered by trees, and to which the inhabitants would bring along the food as soon as ever cooked, so that the visitors should not be annoyed by the prying propensities of the village children, or any other inconvenience! They were extremely exact in all the conventionalities, and a great deal of ceremonial palaver was always gone through at the presentation of the food by the inhabitants, as well as all manner of excuses and apologies for the smallness and bad quality of the same—declaring that it had been a very bad season for the yams, or the pigs somehow or other did not thrive as formerly, and the fish by some inexplicable cause were very chary of being captured, or that they had been of late quite harassed by the multiplicity of visitors, and their having very little to give them grieved them very much—the recipients making answer from time to time by calling aloud "Diva! diva!"—true, true,—and finally they begged to be excused for both quantity and quality, bad cookery, as well as its tardiness in coming along, etc., etc., the visitors making appropriate answers aloud all the time in the shape of "Segai sara," "Kakua"—meaning Not at all! Don't mention it! etc.

I used generally on my first landing to make for the nearest Fiji settlement, instead of following the Tongans to their reception houses, carrying with me a quantity of cutlery and knick-knacks, for the purpose of raking up all the tortoiseshell, mats, native baskets, clubs, spears, shells, wooden pillows, combs, women's native dresses, marked and plain tappa, heads of hair or wigs, head-dresses of both descriptions, brown and white—the colour of the first being caused by a system of smoking—and purchase all these things whilst the food was being prepared by the villagers, and where I was sure to meet with them all of heap, as it were, before they dispersed and got separated on their ordinary avocations. And one morning at the island of "Moce" (Mothy) after finishing the trading and returning from the village to the Tongans, and feeling quite peckish, in consequence of having been all the previous night at sea in the raw air, I found that the ovens had been off some time, and the Tongans had finished their repast, but had reserved for me my ordinary share. It was in a newly plaited coco-nut basket. They pointed it out to me, saying, "There is your portion." I took the basket up and sitting down placed it before me, and proceeded to haul out the contents, which consisted of nicely cooked yams, taro,[1] and breadfruit, each sort being separated from the other by fresh, clean breadfruit leaves, in different layers, one above the other. There was also some Fiji butter, made from the old coco-nut cream, and nicely baked, so that it looked, and tasted somewhat too, like custard; but I was in a very bad humour, and if it is true that passion is the whetstone of courage, I must have been all my lifetime a very courageous man, because the whetstone has been in incessant use with me now for nearly seventy years! I continued to haul these things out one by one, without speaking a word, all eyes being upon me. After

[1] Taro: tuber of a species of Arum.

174

the basket was empty, I took it up and shook it in
a very savage manner, something like a disappointed
dog, looking, or pretending to look, for what I could
not find—pork! Uluqalala asked me very mildly—as
was his wont—what I was looking for? when my
pent-up ill-humour found vent in a torrent of abuse!
I told him that it was no wonder that no white men
ever condescended to live with the Tongans, and
especially their chief, seeing that the Fiji chiefs
were in such plenty, the disparity of treatment being
so notoriously conspicuous, and no wonder that the
latter had conferred the disgraceful sobriquets of
land-sharks on the whole race of Tongans; but had
it been left to me, now that I had found them out,
I should have found a more appropriate name for
them, and then he asked what that name would have
been? I told him it *should* have been *"hogs"!*

At this all the grown-up girls very generously as
well as exceedingly opportunely—I being, as usual,
still a favourite with the fair sex—declared that I
was in this great tantrum of mine on account of my
share of pork being this time forgotten—"puaka"
being the generic name for hogs, pigs, or suckers,
alive or dead, or even pork, salted or fresh, cooked
or raw—ignoring altogether that I had called the

whole box and dice of them "hogs," including the chief, or else I don't know how it would have fared with me for so grossly insulting the chief with all his relations—most of the people present being such —but as usual these pretty things carried the day, and effectually put to silence the clamorous bucks by a double share of clamour, declaring that the word "puaka" was used by me in reference to my forgotten share of that commodity, when one and all burst out in a very loud fit of laughter, I joining, swearing by might and main that the ladies were perfectly correct! because I had been accustomed, I said, my whole life, and my father, grandfather, and great-grandfather, in fact for many generations past, time immemorial, in common with all other white people, especially English ones, to meat three or four times a day, omitting, of course, to qualify this sweeping statement by hinting, in the slightest degree, that hundreds, nay, millions, of the inhabitants of the too much boasted England thought themselves extremely lucky if they tasted butcher-meat once a year, or that the very poor of this much-vaunted country generally looked forward in anticipation of a possible sheep's head and pluck crossing their lips at Christmas time!

CANNIBAL JACK

The chief then apologized for the young men's oversight and promised that such a thing should never happen again, and it never did, for whenever I was absent, on my return to the house, I always found my share of pork—generally a leg —hung right in the doorway, so that I was agreeably reminded by striking my head against it, that there had been "puaka" on hand that day!

In respect to the numerous relations of some of these chiefs, I must here state that their very dignity and power, too, hinges on that fact, and especially in all the Friendly Islands and even Samoa or Navigators' Islands—relations being styled "kaiga" in the former and "aiega" in the latter—and these two terms respectively, preceded by the word "numerous," are always considered synonymous with power and dignity too!

And so in this manner I continued—notwithstanding my occasional outspokenness, and which was quite in keeping with the very robust jocular character of these people—in close friendship with this exceedingly good-meaning chief, and, at last,

CANNIBAL JACK

I got him to introduce me to Josiah, *alias* Lauji, king
George's brother, who was bound to Tonga—when
I say "introduced," that was merely conventional,
as there was no such a thing required, because I
might have done it myself without the slightest introduction or ceremony with any of these most
obliging and hospitable people, and especially the
chiefs—they not being white people, excepting in
their hearts, consequently never refuse—and I feel
fully persuaded never will—to oblige when applied
to, whether one is in distress or not—as was the case
with the captain of the *Triton,* missionary schooner,
to whom I had just previously applied to for a passage to Vavao, as my life was in danger in Fiji, I
told him, and he told me that he was sorry for me,
but that his vessel was not at all adapted for hawk-
ing the likes of me about! I had told him that I
would be quite satisfied to take a deck passage, as
exposure was of but little consequence in the tropics
for a day or two at the most, as it was then blowing
a fair wind, and that I would provision myself and
pay besides; but all this had not the slightest effect
upon him, he being white—as I just remarked—all
over, excepting his heart, and that was black, like
a great many more of the *soi-disant* philanthropic

178

gentry in this world! His refusal meant, as plain as words could have said, that I might be killed and eaten too, and go to perdition afterwards, for all he cared!

And now I bid adieu to Uluqalala and never saw him more, for a few years afterwards I heard that he had departed this life; and although a compromise between heathen and Christian interment was celebrated by his followers, the process of which I fully described before, yet I feel confident that he is *now*—according to St. Luke's version—receiving the just reward of his good gifts, which he so liberally bestowed upon his fellow-creatures, myself being a recipient to no inconsiderable extent.

I embarked with Josiah and his numerous crew in his very large canoe, this being the third and last trial I had undergone in order to reach the Tonga or Friendly Islands, and this time with success, leaving the Fijis behind me to the westward, and cheating the redoubtable but great Cakobau—then in the pride of his strength—of his much-longed-for feed of white "bakola"!

But I must admit, in extenuation of this propensity, that there were faults on both sides, no doubt preponderating considerably on my own side, because what business had I, in reality, to mix or interfere in native wars and politics at all?

But such was the case, and for such intermeddling, I for more than a dozen times as near as d——n it became food for the cannibals, and if I had, it would have been no more than I richly deserved; but kind Providence ruled it otherwise, and for which I hope I am exceedingly grateful!

We passed between the only two high islands in the Hapai group—Tofua and Kaau—and then proceeded on to Tugua, where Mr. Webb's mission station was situated. We were duly received and entertained by the natives of all the islands we touched at according to their usual wont, and perhaps with a little more attention than ordinary on account of Josiah being the king's brother, and also, perhaps, because he was a chief belonging to the village of Lefuka—the capital of the group—situated on the island of the same name, and which place we eventually reached.

On our arrival at the somewhat picturesque village of Lefuka—picturesque, in respect to the long, shady avenue above high-water mark, formed by a number of short kind of coco-nut tree, all bearing most prolifically, so that one could help himself from just above his head as he walked along this most delicious retreat.

King George, *alias* Tupo, or Tuekanokopulu, was now being feasted by his subjects of the Hapai group—the third group which he ruled—to wit, this one, Vavao, and Tonga Laki or Amsterdam, and all through his own prowess, he being a *bona fide* warrior among a nation of warriors. He owned a palace in each capital of each group, built in European style by European mechanics. This one was situated in the midst of a nice park-like piece of flat grassy ground, planted with flowers, creepers, and shrubs, and divided into tasty sections by raised, white, sandy paths, and all surrounded by a very neat ornamental reed fence, which was likely to last in good repair for years, as the lower part of it was constantly being weeded by the different gangs of short-sentenced youths for venial offences.

There were two Wesleyan missionaries at this place, and, as the contents of the feast were spread out on a nice green, one of them made his appearance, strolling about at his leisure, merely to have a look, I suppose. His name was Raborne, and was a stout, strong, bluff, lusty-looking man of nearly or quite forty years of age, and of the regular John

Bull type. King George called to him, and as he approached said, "Misi Lepone"—take notice there is no sound of the letters r or b in the Tongan language—"send along a knife." This knife was required to carve one of the best cooked hogs as a kind of preliminary luncheon whilst the big feast was in preparation, and also a kind of crust after the "kava," which was then being prepared in three or four immense round shallow dishes called "tanoas," when he made answer that he had better use the knives that his mother had used before him! meaning split pieces of bamboo! He now came up to where I was sitting cross-legged, Turkish or tailor fashion, beside the king, and accosted me very brusquely, asking me where I had so suddenly sprung from? and, no doubt, he thought me, if not exactly a very disreputable character, a very eccentric one, at very least! and well he might, seeing I had neither shirt nor trousers on me, only just a fathom of thin white calico round my loins—a garb I had adopted for coolness—and I returned the compliment, albeit unknown to himself, unless there is a great deal of truth in "thought language," and I am inclined to believe there may be, by mentally estimating him as an extremely rough character, and especially for a missionary!

We got into conversation, when, among other things, he asked me, which of the two races—Tonga or Fiji—I thought the most clever? I said, in respect to ingenuity, I decidedly gave the latter the preference. He said he wished to goodness they would exercise a little more of it, clothing themselves with a little more decency when they came about his premises—the Fijians leave the hind parts completely bare,—before he should be necessitated to teach them a palpable lesson they would not easily forget!

Just at this moment, as the king's share of three or four of the largest hogs were deposited on the grass in front of where he was sitting, I immediately, quite unceremoniously, jumped up and clapped my right hand on the heap, when they were as quickly borne off to Josiah's house by five or six of the younger men of our canoe's crew, and then Mr. Raborne retired, and I believe this short and casual interview tended to mutually impress, for a time at any rate, an unfavourable decision in regard to each of our characters!

The fact of me so cavalierly seizing the whole of

the king's share of cooked hogs as well as vegetables, etc., was a prerogative enjoyed by any foreigner who happened to be on hand at the time, and
had been introduced by this very generous monarch,
in the same way that he had made public, that all
foreigners could take young coco-nuts, whenever
and wherever they happened to be overtaken by
thirst, throughout the whole length and breadth
of all his dominions; and yet not one of the score or
more residing in the three groups scarcely, if ever,
availed himself of this privilege, through ignorance
or perhaps disinclination, but I had learned the
"ropes" as well as the language of this very interesting people long before this.

When I repaired to Josiah's house, and now my
home, the natives proposed to me that it was best
to cook them over again, as the first cooking is
hardly ever more than warmed through at any of
these big feasts, quantity being the sentiment rather
than quality at nearly all the gigantic banquets.
When I say *gigantic* they well deserved that adjectival appellation, for I suppose it will scarcely be cred-
ited by the reader when I state that at some of these
banquets there were a thousand cooked pigs, big and
little, brought on to the green at once, with other

things in proportion, and that every day consecutively, sometimes prolonged to the extent of ten days or even a fortnight; but then they were always conducted at the respective capitals of the three groups —to wit, Niafu at Vavao, Lefuka at the Hapais, and Nukualofa at Tongatabu—and then of course all the outlying provinces had to contribute whenever this new king put in an appearance on his periodical round from group to group; but then he was at that time but recently established, and the first man, I suppose, who had ever ruled the whole of the Friendly Islands, each group hitherto being ruled by separate individual chiefs, and sometimes, no doubt, by a number of chiefs, and so we must not wonder much at the prodigality of these small islands, it being on the principle of a new broom sweeping clean, but then King George's broom has been sweeping for the last half-century and that pretty clean too!

When the natives proposed to cook these hogs over again, I knew that if I allowed it to be carried into effect, they would all be devoured at one meal by these very hearty trencher-men, and as I wished to see something more of the brusque missionary, I accordingly spruced myself up by donning a clean white shirt and trousers, a brand-new black silk tie round my neck, a pair of new slippers and white cotton socks, and Manilla hat—things I generally kept on hand, when possible, for a stand-by—and then wrapped four very large pieces of turtleshell in a new piece of clean white calico, and forthwith proceeded up to His Reverence's residence—making a virtue of a necessity—knocking quite a respectful knock at the door, which brought Mr. Raborne himself to open it. He looked as if taken quite aback with surprise, for the moment, at the metamorphosis, I suppose; but he as quickly recovered himself, when he escorted me into the presence of his wife and children, all of whom received me very graciously. After having quite a gossip, principally about missionaries I had left behind me in Fiji, most of whom they knew, I begged of the lady to accept the shell as a token of my deep regard to missionary people at large, and an earnest of my future respect to herself and husband in particular. When I left, I found myself in possession of a large, clean, empty cask, and enough salt for salting the whole of my pigs; besides, they both insisted upon sending a couple of male-servants to convey these things to my home for me.

CANNIBAL JACK

I now took employment from Mr. Raborne, which as soon as ever he learned from my conversation that I was a handy-man he offered me. I found that he was all that my first impression had taught me to believe regarding his character, or rather, perhaps, idiosyncrasy, that is, to say the very least, he was rough, and exceedingly outspoken, as a sample of which I remember that in using a plane—it was a jack-plane—which I had put in order as well as all the rest of a chest of his new tools, that he corrected me in no very polite manner for the way in which I drew it back over the wood, declaring that I would spoil the face of it, when I immediately substituted the plan of canting it on to one of its lower side edges, drawing it back in that manner; but neither did this suit him, because he said these lower edges were often called into requisition by *real* mechanics to test the trueness of the work they were performing, when I told him that one being willing at all times, like myself, to be instructed, often got into various habits, some of them, of course, decidedly wrong, and then he took the plane from me, and after making one planing motion, drew it back on the edge of its further lower front end, but it was evident to me that *he* was not, at any rate, a "real"

187

mechanic! As I was planing away, the natives—some of whom were almost constantly round, and especially when anything more than ordinary, as now, was taking place—generally stuck themselves right in the way, at the further end of the bench, and Mr. Raborne observing this, said, "Jack, did you never hear the yarn about the cobbler,—how, when he was drawing out his wax-ends to their full length, struck one of the onlookers several taps in the stomach, till at last one of these being harder than the previous ones, consequently caused considerable pain, when he immediately jumped out of the way, saying I see I am in your way. Not at all said the cobbler, if you are not in your own way, you are not in mine." "And now, Jack, if you will serve these natives in the same way with the end of the plane they will soon get out of their own way as well as yours, and I also shall be much obliged to you!"

I did all manner of jobs for this very bluff Englishman and blunter missionary, and one day he proposed that I should copy off a manuscript book of sermons, written by himself in the Tongan language, so that each of his teachers could have a copy at each of their homes on the different islands in the group. He asked, "What I would take per copy for the whole job?" I told him since he had left it to myself to decide, I thought that two pounds per book would be a fair thing between man and master, as there were just a hundred sermons in the original, and that I could write eight sermons a day by a little extra exertion, so that it would be a tight fortnight's work, consequently a pound a week for my trouble. At this his outspokenness stood him in good stead, for he declared that, as the first copy had been intended for Joele, the Governor of Hapai—it being missionary policy as a general thing to get the chiefs to be leaders in the religious cause as well as in a lay point of view, and I think very good policy too— but he said if that was to be the price of it, he would see Master Joele hung—hung as high as Gilderoy, first, and besides, he said, that writing was a gentleman's work compared to carpentering, sometimes outside exposed to the hot sun, etc., etc.; and so, on second consideration, I eventually agreed to take thirty shillings per copy, seeing that I was to live at his table, which although very little to him, a great deal to me, because the food would be properly prepared, good, clean, and regular, which is more than can be said when one is obliged to be satisfied

with the native larder—which is among all natives
either a feast or a famine!

I continued to work on for Mr. Raborne, he feeding me like a fighting-cock all the time, lending me
books—generally religious—or always, to say the
very least, with a good moral, he never omitting to
write on the fly-leaf, that he hoped that it would
prove a blessing to me! And when I had done all
his work he offered to pay me in hard cash, or if I
preferred—as cash was not in those early times in
general circulation, and especially among the natives
—I could have it in kind or "trade," asking me what
sort I wished to have. I told him that I preferred
large knives, because I knew that a dollar knife
would purchase from the natives a hog which two
dollars' worth of print would not secure. Mr. Raborne also knew this as well, if not better, than I
did; but still he distressed himself by complying with
my request, and even had to go to his colleague, who
lived next door, depriving themselves, as they only
received their supplies once in two years from the
Mission's schooner, *Triton,* at that time.

This precious jewel of a man departed this life
up in the colonies a few years afterwards—the best
of men, it seems to me, we always lose first! His

CANNIBAL JACK

field of labour, I think, was on the Hunter, because
I remember seeing in some paper or pamphlet a
short sketch about his chiding some of the effemi-
nate ones in a boat with him, when he jumped out,
up to his knees in water, saying, that's the way we
do it down at the islands! It may be said by some of
my readers that they are all good fellows who give
me things. A much wiser than myself said, "A
gift in secret pacifieth anger; and a reward in the
bosom strong wrath"—Raborne, as I said above,
was a precious jewel set in a rough casket!

I now converted all these knives and the rest of
the things I had received from Mr. Raborne, together with the trade which was left of my Fiji
stock, into large hogs and pigs of every conceivable
size and condition, and of both sexes, and then paid
the natives for erecting a strong, high, circular
fence inclosing a large space of ground, had large
sheds for shelter put up inside, and sunk canoes in
different parts for the swine to eat and drink from,
bought old coco-nuts in tens of thousands, paid boys
for breaking down the branches of certain trees,
whose green leaves are very succulent, and which
pigs very greedily devour, and straight away turned

pig-jobber, breeder, etc. Ah! those were the times, no competition, had it all my own way!

I NOW made a trip in a sailing canoe to Vavao— no passage to pay, the natives being too glad of my company—leaving people in charge of my stock.

When I arrived at headquarters (Niafu), I found that the island was labouring under very heavy convulsions of earthquake shocks, forty odd of which were marked down by a missionary lady in one single day!

I went on board an American whaler which had just come to anchor. Everything on board was completely covered—yards, masts, sails, decks—by a greyish kind of impalpable dust, and on inquiring the cause, was told by one of the chaps, "that when their ship was two degrees to windward of Tonualei—an island, perhaps, some thirty miles from Vavao—the captain called all hands, and ordered them to man their shovels and put in as tight as they could dig to save the ship from sinking!" Taking this to be merely a Yankee yarn, I inquired further —of the captain himself this time—when he par-

tially corroborated this statement, accounting for
the somewhat phenomenal fall of dust to *windward*
of the site of the irruption, by supposing that the
force of the hitherto pent-up explosion had driven it
through the lower current of air into an upper one,
which was then operating in the exact opposite direction. Several of the then white residents with
myself now took a boat and went to Tonualei, and
when we reached it, one of the most sublime as well
as most terrific sights presented itself which it is
possible to conceive.

The island, which had before been completely
clothed with verdure, was now one mass of gravel,
ashes, and lava! The crater, which seemed too big
for the island, was belching and vomiting, ejecting
stones, rocks, as well as all manner of combustible
matter. We essayed to land, but had to beat a precipitate retreat to the boat again, because it was impossible to keep our feet on the shore, and it would
have been extremely dangerous to have remained
over a few seconds, lest we should have never gained
the boat again, on account of a kind of heart-sick
dizziness, something akin to sea-sickness but three
times as virulent! As it was, one of our chaps was
with great difficulty rescued, and did not thoroughly

recover his wonted strength and elasticity till we reached Vavao on our return!

But now that we had arrived at Niafu the whole of the shock all over Vavao had completely subsided, the volcano at Tonualei acting as a safety-valve for the whole of the Vavao group, in the same way as the volcano on Tofua does for the Hapai group, I should suppose.

This Tonualei is the real island, whence originated that beautiful, romantic, traditionary story of the two lovers and their cave home, entered by diving under water from the sea, and mentioned by Mariner in his *Account of the Tongan Islands,* and whence also Lord Byron, with a poet's license, transferred the scene of "The Island" in his poetic works to another country and distinct people (the Tahitians), verging on a distance of a thousand miles, helped also by the assistance of Lieutenant Bligh's *Narrative of the Mutiny and Seizing of the "Bounty" in the South Seas, in* 1789—now just a century ago. What changes! millions upon millions!! even to me in my own little world, during my short peregrinations of a little over half a century, to say nothing of a whole one!!!

About this time the French were very busy at

CANNIBAL JACK

Tahiti, trying to pacify the natives so as to introduce their protectorate into the group, and as the troops were sometimes reduced to quite short commons in respect to provisions, and especially of the fresh-meat kind, there was quite a trade extemporized out of that port by the small craft, for the purpose of supplying the defect, by purchasing pigs at the various adjacent groups, and one of these vessels called at the harbour of Niafu at Vavao.

The captain and owner was a Frenchman, his crew a mixed one—composed of English, Dutch, Spanish, etc., etc.,—consequently, as usual, not congenial, excepting on one subject, and that was, "that they would go no further in the old rattle-trap because she was not seaworthy!" they said. I became acquainted with the little oldish captain, and he told me that he was meeting with very bad luck in this my adopted country, as he called it, inasmuch as the "big pigs were eating the little ones!"—a fact, because the foolish fellow had mixed them all together, and had not given them a sufficiency of food, and of course they had turned cannibals, and this was the third cargo, I think, he said, that he had purchased, and still the thing went on in the same way as in the beginning. He, clapping his hand on his

breast with the tears in his eyes, said "he was like
the other man, because he did not like the monish"
—albeit he had plenty of it for his present use at
any rate, for he hauled six drawers out chockfull of
the dollars of as many different nationalities—to
wit, Old Spanish, Bolivian, Peruvian, American,
Mexican, and French five-franc pieces, declaring
that if I would assist him to the utmost of my power,
that I would find him a liberal paymaster. I accordingly, with the assistance of a couple of chums I
had on shore, went to work and divided the whole
of the hold into different strong, rough compart-
ments of different sizes, according to requirement,
and bought some thousand of old coco-nuts, besides
giving the pigs plenty of green stuff whilst we were
replenishing the cargo. We then also held a survey
over the vessel and pronounced her seaworthy, providing certain repairs were gone through with, and
which repairs we ourselves did quite to the satisfaction of the Frenchman, and then obliged the crew
by the assistance of the native authorities on shore
to return to their duty, although greatly against
their wills, and for all this trouble and work I received from the captain six hundred dollars, two
hundred of which I gave to my two helps, and for

which they were exceedingly pleased, because it did not often happen that men of their description could so easily pick up a hundred dollars each on such an island as Vavao—this being quite a windfall to them.

I now concluded that this Vavao was a much more eligible place to settle down in than the Hapais, on account of its consequent shipping—the shipping consisting principally of whalers, and the most of them American, with a small percentage of London, French, and Colonial ditto, and so I betook myself back to Lefuka and sold out to Mr. J. Williams— son of the *then* late great J. Williams, pioneer missionary, killed and devoured by the savages of Dillon's Bay, Eromanga, New Hebrides—who was down in a schooner of his own from Apia, Samoa, where he was British Consul, for the purpose of purchasing pigs for the whalers, touching at those islands for fresh provisions; but as the feasting for King George was constantly going on, there happened to be a "tabu" or veto put on to all the grunters, in order to supply the almost constant demand, and he—Mr. W.—the more readily, rather than go back empty-handed, bought me out.

I sold him two hundred pigs of various sizes, together with all my tortoiseshell, clubs, spears, mats, native tappa, native mosquito screens, fancy wooden pillows, women's grass dresses, shells, baskets, native carved dishes, and bowls, etc., etc.,—in fact, all and everything, in the shape of curiosities, useful and ornamental, which I possessed, and for which I received a considerable deal more than a thousand dollars, and then made straight back to Vavao, where I had a house built and took as a partner an old Yankee ex-boatsteerer who happened to be a blacksmith by trade, started a forge and made hoes and spears for cultivating the ground and capturing fish, both of which the natives readily purchased at a good price for pigs, as the "tabu" was now off. We also established a carpenter's shop, sawed our own wood, principally of the hard-wood "fetau" species, and which made excellent ornamental dovetailed chests, but the planing of it had to be done by tooth-planes on account of the extraordinary crooked grain of this famous wood; but then our labour was not in vain, because the natives readily gave fifteen dollars for each chest, when they happened to have the cash, and if not, an equivalent. Our establishment consumed more food in the shape of pigs, goats, turkeys, ducks, fowls, eggs, fish,

CANNIBAL JACK

yams, taro, breadfruit, bananas, and all other kinds
of fruit indigenous to the tropics, besides European
provisions, not excepting wines, ales, and ardent
spirits, although the latter was strictly forbidden,
even to be landed, by the missionary laws,—I say,
more was consumed in one day by old Joe and myself, including the hangers-on in the shape of servants or "helps," in those good old times, than any
hotel in either Levuka or Suva in Fiji, or Noumea in
New Caledonia, consumes in a week in these degen-
erate times!

I HAVE not this morning—the last day of July,
1889—I am sorry to say, the requisite *cacoethes
scribendi,* neither have I had for months past; but as
I have no earthly way of amusing myself or anyone
to amuse, I suppose I may as well continue the
paper-spoiling business whether willing or not, and
so, to resume the old subject, "my life," I may as well
state, that although I did what I should have *then*
called my "business" in Vavao, yet I must here remark that it is not all gold which glitters; but as I
was then young, consequently buoyant, I thought—
i.e. if I, at that time, thought at all—that I was

actually performing a great stroke, indeed, with my pack upon my back strolling from village to village, purchasing pigs from the natives.

It must be borne in mind by the reader, notwithstanding what I have hitherto related regarding the good qualities of the natives at large, throughout the length and breadth of the Friendly Islands, that they had a terrible large quantity of alloy, *alias* deviltry, in their compositions, and especially those of this particular part—the Vavaos being the black spot of the three groups. In going along the paths I would sometimes meet three or four rowdies—there being no lack of larrikins here any more than there was in Sydney, and especially in Pitt Street, at that time!

These gentlemen would commence with assumed civility and then speedily shift their tactics into fulsome chaff, banter, etc.; and if these did not succeed in irritating me, they would have recourse to stronger measures well known to savages as well as uncouth whites! These measures consisted in pulling my bundle at my back, sometimes toppling me over on top of it! and then, as all patience was now completely exhausted, I would up and challenge the ablest among them to a pugilistic encounter, and if luckily getting the best of him, another would step in—manliness not being in the ascendancy with these wretches—notwithstanding their supposed missionary teaching, and then, one or more of the disengaged curs would run off with the bundle!

But I did not get bitten in these games more than once or twice, for ever afterwards I took the initiative, by commencing *myself* to bully and bluster these infernal upstart imps, who made a regular practice of waylaying me! I generally knew pretty well where they had secreted themselves, and, under the pretence of firing at birds, I used to let strip all around them, without a moment's warning, with my double-barrelled fowling-piece and pistols, reserving, however, some of my arms undischarged for self-defence; but the cowardly villains had no notion of converting a comedy into a tragedy, but always scampered off, crashing the bushes down at a great rate, frightened out of their very wits if not exactly their skins!

When I arrived in the villages, I always stipulated that I would purchase their pigs on one condition only, and that was, that each one should convey his sold pig or pigs to Niafu by the expiration of a certain date, specified in their own language, in a blank book, which I always carried with me for the purpose, making each one sign his name, if he could, or else attach his mark, before I paid him. Many of them used to give false names, and which again just answered my purpose, for I would then pull them at court under a charge of fraudulent attempts, obtaining goods under false pretences, etc., etc., generally receiving two pigs for one—not that these laws were much in vogue at the time, but through me being so extremely insistent in the matter, rather than prolong the discussion, which was never very agreeable to the self-sufficient judge, I generally carried my point, and eventually that became the established penalty for these particular offences.

These courts were, at that time, in many respects, a mere farce, the prosecutor and witnesses never being sworn on the Bible, till I introduced the formula. It came about in the following manner: One night, in returning from a village where I had gone to on a visit, for the purpose of drinking "kava" (the intoxicating beverage) with the old gentlemen of the place—and who, by the by, are always extremely kind and hospitable, and especially to a white who, like myself, can converse fluently with them in their own language. On leaving at about ten o'clock p.m., I bid them all good night, which they all responded to in a most friendly manner, excepting one young black called "Netane," and he *overdid* the thing, creating a strong suspicion at once in my breast, by calling out very lustily, and rowdily, too, three distinct times, "Good night, Jack," and even after I was well on the road home —a distance of not quite a mile—I still heard his voice, and also the hoarse laugh of the other larrikins of the village! I pulled foot as fast as I could without actually running, knowing something was up! but it appeared this rascal pulled foot a great deal faster, for he got ahead of me, notwithstanding that he had to go round through the bush, leaving the beaten path, in order to cut me off.

When about half-way home I descried a native ahead of me coming towards me. There was a little moon, I had no firearms with me, but I had a very formidable dirk which I always carried about my person. It occurred at once to me that this man could be no other than Netane, and that he meant murdering me through sheer wantonness, incited also, perhaps, by jealousy. I met him, and although the road was broad here, I did not try to avoid him, knowing that it was useless; but as soon as ever I was abreast of him—we being some five or six feet apart—I made one sudden spring right up alongside of him—knowing that if he had a club I should be safer close to him than a few feet apart. I had my dirk unsheathed and in my right hand, but in a way that I thought he could not see it, but I saw that he had a club in his right hand, and which he tried to conceal from me by keeping his body between it and myself as it hung down along his right side. Each of our left sides were in contact, so that he could not use the club at present, we being too close together. I grasped his left wrist with my left hand as we almost faced each other, saying, "Is this Netane?" He was trembling, and so, thinking perhaps he had thought better of it in his fear, which I took the trembling to indicate, I demanded again if it was Netane, when he said, "Yes!" I then said, "What are you doing here, then?" I then made the same kind of sudden spring away from him as I had done in approaching him, in order to be out of the reach of his club, and then said, "Good night, Netane"; but he swung his unoccupied left hand on to his club, and now with both hands and a rush he made a swinging blow at my head, which I avoided by dodging my head, but received the blow across the shoulders, without, however, it hurting me very much.

I omitted to relate just now, in its proper place, perhaps, but better late than never, and so I will relate it now: just after I left the village, and whilst Netane was going round through the bushes in order to get ahead of me, there were two others— his accomplices—following me behind in order to inclose me between Nathan and themselves, so as to make doubly sure of their prey. I heard them whispering at my heels, but did not even turn round to accost them, or mend my pace, lest by these means I should betray symptoms of fear, and thereby give these curs Dutch courage to commence the attack; but I said, as I proceeded on at a quick walking pace, "Mind what you are up to!" "Remember the Tong-atabu affair!" This affair alluded to a Tongan in the last-mentioned place, who was escorting a white Portuguese, through the low scrub in broad daylight, when he lifted his club to dash his brains out; but the Portuguese perceiving the shadow of the club caused by the meridian sun, just had time, and nothing to spare, to turn on his heel and confront this would-be assassin and as quick as lightning sheathed his knife in his abdomen before the club descended on his head, and then cut a blazing star, scattering his entrails all about the ground, and also got clear down to the boat, which was a good distance off, notwithstanding the fact of his having to rush through a big mob of the mutilated one's compatriots, who were doing their utmost to intercept him so as to, of course, kill him, showing this very self-opinionated race that there were other smart people in the world as well as themselves! He got safely to his ship and well he deserved to do so! I also remarked that I was not only a white, but an English white! These remarks caused these two villains to hang back.

When "Netane" struck me over the shoulder instead of the head as he intended, instead of letting me pass as I had shown him the example of letting well alone, by refraining to butcher him when I had him by the wrist, discovering at the same time that he had, almost, remarkably small bones, and which I had before observed by daylight—when I said, "And now I will kill you," and rushed at him to do so, but he bolted back again towards his village and I after him; but I soon found that I was rushing into a trap, for I now espied two other natives— his accomplices, of course, and the same two who had just previously hung back. Netane now began calling out, "Here he is!" meaning me, as his courage began to revive on again seeing these two fellows.

And now came my turn to bolt, and which I did as fast as my legs would carry me, right back to my own village of Utue; but I need not have been in such a hurry, for I found that they did not follow me. As soon as I arrived, I called out all the male inhabitants and demanded that they should accompany me back, and which they most readily did, as the whole of the inhabitants of this Utue were under a great obligation to me, inasmuch as I had made it my business, for the last six months past, to clothe men, women, and children gratis, in order to secure their friendship, because I had made this village, *pro tem.*, my country residence for the sake of trading, and I also was endeavouring to secure for myself a female helpmate as a substitute for poor Litia whom I had buried in Fiji.

After well arming myself—with firearms this time—we all returned to the village of the would-be murderers. When we arrived these young villains were as busy as ever they could be singing religious hymns, beefing out at the very top of their voices,

Netane leading—a mere ruse, of course, to blind the older, consequently the more respectable portion of the inhabitants. Whilst my gang were arguing the pro and con of this most diabolical assault, I was busy punching Master Netane, telling him at the same time that had he had aught against me, he ought to have challenged me to a pugilistic encounter as he was twice my size, and especially considering that the Tongan larrikins hold themselves to be quite *au fait* at this most reputable accomplishment, and continually boast about it in disparagement of the youths of all other nations with whom they are acquainted; and as for the smartness of whites, of course that bears not the slightest comparison to their own! I told him that he ought to have done that instead of trying to murder me in such a treacherous and cowardly manner, and especially in these times of law and order, but that now it was too late, because the time had gone by, and if he offered to retaliate with his fists or even run away, I would now blow his brains out with the pistol I held in my left hand full cocked; whilst I thus held him *in terrorism* with one hand, I punched his ugly mug with the other to my heart's content. When I had done with him I don't think Maata—the bone of contention, it seems, between us—would have preferred his lordship—he being one of the "lords of the soil"—to my humble self, albeit I was but an insignificant stranger in their paltry country!

As soon as this villain's disfiguration had cleared off, I had him arrested and escorted down to the court held at Niafu to answer the charge of an intended capital offence.

A fellow who acted in the triple capacity of governor, ordained minister of the gospel, and judge, albeit not fit for any of the three, seeing that he was prejudiced to a most abnormal extent against the foreigner, and prepossessed in favour of his countrymen. I appeared as prosecutor and insisted to be sworn on the Bible, and especially as I had no witnesses, and that my evidence was, after all, but circumstantial, seeing that I could not have positively sworn to Netane's identity in the partial light of that night's small moon, when the attack took place; but I swore "to the best of my belief," dwelling on the fact of his paying his addresses to Maata as well as many other females at the time, and then to the significance of his bidding me "good night" three distinct times and in such a rowdy style, when once sufficed for everybody else, which fact, in itself alone, conveyed a threat, I said, and that the intended assault was further corroborated by the very pronounced horse laugh of the rest of the larrikins congregated with himself in a house by themselves, and all this happening but ten minutes previous to my receiving the blow from the club, added to all the above came the trembling when I took hold of his wrist—a guilty conscience wanting no accusing, I said. I also drew the attention of the court to the smallness of his wrist-bones—a thing the more remarkable with a race who are generally famous for large bones,—besides, his making back to his own village when I chased him, went to show that he belonged to that village and no other, there being several others hard by and paths leading thereto; I maintained that he was making back to his accomplices after being too precipitate in striking me before these other two fellows had had time to rally and come up and so enclose me, and had they done so I should have been obliged to have shown myself exceedingly smart with my dirk, and lucky should I have been had I escaped with my life or at least without being severely wounded!

This heaven-born judge quibbled and argued in favour of the prisoner at the Bar, who had pleaded "not guilty," and would certainly have discharged him, had it not been for the fact of me insisting and persisting, in cross-questioning the prisoner so closely, and much to the disgust of this very immaculate judge—so much so, indeed, that this infallible administrator of the law actually forgot that he was a preacher of the Gospel, and even jumped up and manned his club which hung on the reed partition over his head, and would, perhaps, have used it on me; but the people cried shame of this proceeding, which brought his lordship to his senses again!

This little episode created a diversion, and the prisoner seeing that the case seemed to be going against him, as I had the sympathy of the whole of the people in court, which was crowded, shifted his tactics, throwing himself on the mercy of the court, by making a clean breast of it, acknowledging that as I was a white man ("papalage") that it was useless still to kick against the pricks, and that he was guilty, and so, by the advice of the people at large, he was sentenced to three years' transportation to the volcanic island of Tonualei to eat crabs when he could catch them, and drink water when kind Providence thought fit to send rain, for his sustenance. In any reasonable court in almost any other part of the world circumstantial evidence against Master Netane would have convicted him even if he had not admitted his guilt as he at the last did, because there were so many corroborating proofs in the chain of evidence, and, lastly if not leastly, there was the peculiar tone of his voice, when he called aloud to his accomplices on coming up to them after clubbing me, and which I swore to—I mean when he called out "Here he is," meaning me! but it never occurred to these would-be lawyers that I had, in a manner, condoned with the prisoner, when I gave him that awful punching, by taking the law into my own hands!

King George suspended the governor from being judge and appointed another in his place, and old Mr. Turner, the *then* missionary at Niafu, suspended him from preaching the Gospel, and all because he had lifted his club at me in court!

A BOUT this time there had been landed an Englishman at Niafu from an American whaler, suffering under an ailment something akin to palpitation of the heart, and he was housed with "Old John," an ex-convict from N.S.W., and seeing that this poor fellow had not the best attendance, and which fact considerably retarded his recovery, I proposed that I would have him conveyed up to my country residence, and which he readily acceded to. In a very short time he was in a state of convalescence, and on his complete recovery I proposed that I would give him all the smaller pigs if he would, in the way of amusing himself, just help me to break up every day the old coco-nuts to feed the whole herd. I did this so that his feelings should not be hurt by thinking that he was under an obligation to me, and also that I should not lose his company, as he was really a nice fellow and quite the gentleman: his name was Powel.

A large canoe had been away on a twelve-month's cruise to all the outlying islands, but most of the time had been spent on the Samoan or Navigators' Islands, a place they used to go to for the purpose of cheating Tuekanokopolu's law by having the much-coveted breeches tattooed on their persons, and which heathen custom had been, some time previous to this, interdicted by this said king, by the advice of the missionaries throughout the Friendly Islands, and so on their return they easily submitted to the fine, knowing that the breeches could not be pulled off again, whereas if they had remained at home they never could have been put on, and then they would run a terrible risk of being estimated in the eyes of the fair sex about the same as if emasculated!

This canoe had returned, and the crew were at their usual occupation, i.e. they were airing their new breeches as well as their consequence by strolling from village to village in that *dolce far niente* style, in which they are such great proficients! They had reached my village of Utue. There was a lady in their company, and she had made the voyage with them, and she alone of the fair sex. This lady —about twenty years of age—was, physically, perfect; morally, very imperfect, inasmuch as it was rumoured that she had rendered herself exceedingly entertaining and obliging to the whole of the eighty young bloods composing the canoe's crew during their twelve months' absence! She came into my house, inviting herself as it were, demanding a jew's harp in that brazen way peculiar to courtesans in general and Tongan ones in particular—there being no public opinion in this country, i.e. not in the way that term is estimated in England, for instance; but, if any at all, quite in the opposite direction, for this class can mix with the virtuous ones—that is, if there are any of the latter, without these latter suffering the slightest detraction on account of the familiarity.

I answered her very abruptly or curtly, which her behaviour fully deserved, and which quite offended quite a number of her paramours. The brother of the transported Netane had strolled up from his village in order to mix with these returned bucks, and was making himself quite conspicuous at my expense, by cracking numbers of my already husked old coco-nuts, in order to get at the sweet kernels—which somewhat resemble sponge cake—and which he was first handing to this lady, and then to the gents. I remarked to this fast gentleman, "that those nuts had been bought, and that the purchaser (myself) was not very far distant!" To this strong hint he paid not the slightest attention, but continued the cracking the nuts, ignoring alike myself and all I said, the lady in ecstasies of delight at the fun, and even my affianced, the irreproachable Maata, then present, was quite tickled at the *sangfroid* of this young spark! I was fast losing all self-control; but when some forty or fifty of this fast fry, consisting of male and female, burst out into an irrepressible laugh—and *such* a laugh! much louder than the tittering that had just preceded it— I could contain myself no longer, but sprung to the native with one bound, calling aloud, *"that they had been paid for too!"* I drove my head and shoulders into the fork of this defiant buck, with almost supernatural force, making him perform as complete a somersault clean over my head, as ever was performed by the most practised gymnastic, and then when grounded, as quick as lightning I stood with both feet on one of his legs, whilst I raised the other with both my hands nearly as high as my head, almost splitting him in twain, and then called to the bystanders, especially the female portion of them, to come and take a good squint at the predicament this particular lady-killer of theirs was in!

This broke up the fun, and, as luck would have it, without, at this bout at any rate, me getting broken up myself, because all these bucks knew well that, had they carried it further, I should have been certain to fly to my firearms, and so they dispersed quite crestfallen, and the does slipped away with a kind of mock modesty, mixed with hardly repressed tittering!

The very next night Miss Maata was missing,

and a search was made throughout all the houses of the adjacent villages and continued through the whole of the next day. It was found that Netane's brother was also absent from home, and, as he had been seen in company with this most virtuous damsel, a search was instituted and carried right away into the heart of the surrounding virgin forest, but not till the fourth or fifth day were they discovered. They had erected themselves a nice little hut as they anticipated ruralizing for quite a lengthened period; but, contrary to their expectations, they were escorted down to Niafu to be tried by the missionary laws for elopement. The girl was advised by her friends to acknowledge the whole of her guilt without reservation, in order that her punishment might be the lighter, and also on the principle of "confession" which they take from holy writ—to wit, where it is said, "Confess your sins to one another."

She admitted that she had sinned—a *little!* And now the judge told her that if she expected leniency of the court she would have to be more explicit, and especially if she wished God's forgiveness, and that that was the place to forgo all squeamishness, because shame itself was utterly misplaced there, and to relate in detail the how and why she had been betrayed into this escapade; besides, as court work was in itself generally dull and monotonous, he should advise her for the sake of making it somewhat interesting, and also that she would acquit herself as a lady, by contributing to the amusement of the great number of ladies and gentlemen congregated in King George's honourable court purposely to be amused. Being thus encouraged she at once made a clean breast of it, and acknowledged that she had committed herself, this last time whilst in the bush, nineteen—perhaps twenty—times, and had anticipated doing it as many hundreds of times, and that was the reason they had built the hut! All this was said amid the great cheering of the whole court—male and female—not excepting the judge himself! She also said that this gentleman, as well as the transported Netane his brother, had been her paramours for eight years; and so, as she was now about eighteen years old, it appears that it is not mere supposition that puberty is hastened by the tropical sun. She continued her confession, enumerating more than forty other sparks with whom she had been in pleasurable consort, telling the *how* it happened to the great amusement of these very licentious people, the details of which would not look well in an English translation on paper, however proper it was in an honourable Tongan court. The rest of her paramours—which were legion—she had forgotten their names; besides, many were dead, she said.

The judge summed up, by telling her, that as she had proved herself so good a girl by giving him so little trouble and so materially contributed to the amusement of the ladies and gentlemen there present, and for their company he took the present opportunity of thanking them most sincerely, and to show his gratitude he left the decision of the duration of her punishment to the ladies and gentlemen present—when they all vociferated, *"A month!" "A month!"* and a month it was instead of a year, had it been left to the judge himself. She was accordingly taken away to beat "tappa" in a very long building erected for the purpose, where she would be in company with scores—sometimes hundreds—of others at the same occupation and for the same offence; hardly any other crime excepting adultery or fornication is even looked into. Their food was generally supposed to be supplied by their relations and often their lovers contributed to no small amount, and whose kindness did not always go unremunerated, and which, if not too glaring, was always winked at by the officials as they participated to a very great extent in favours of more than one description; and as for the higher authorities they did not wish to be pestered about these minor matters—the missionaries had finished their task when they promulgated the laws and troubled themselves no further about them, and the king and chiefs of course had done their full share when they signed and ratified them, long since!

Maata's present lover during the boisterous paroxysms of mirth at the trial, not being particularly guarded—in fact, he was enjoying the fun quite as much as the spectators—had embraced the opportunity of absconding; and that very night, as I lay reading to my mate, Powel, by a coco-nut-shell lamp at my head, the venetian blind kind of mat striced up all round the sides of the house for the sake of air, I received a stone aimed at my head; but, lucky for me, it missed that mortal part and struck me on the left shoulder. We now went in search of this would-be murderer, captured him, and the next day conveyed him to Niafu. A special court was extemporized for the occasion, and although the judge quibbled at first, I soon brought him to a better understanding, he remembering that his predecessor had been ousted principally through my means. He was convicted and packed off to keep his brother Netane's company at Fonualea, without much ceremony. Before starting, however, he admitted his guilt.

THE missionaries had had a terrible job with this self-sufficient, wild, uncouth race, and especially a few years previous to my arrival in the country, for it was next to impossible for the latter to be sufficiently schooled to brook control, they being arrogant and prejudiced to the last degree. They despised a foreigner, and took not the slightest care to disguise that feeling, but embraced every opportunity of exhibiting their utmost aversion. They wondered what business foreigners had in their country at all, introducing new laws which so much interfered with their hitherto free and easy life.

* * * *

In respect to King George's courage, had he lacked it, he never would have entered the position he now holds, nor would he have retained it as he has for the last half-century. In respect to his sense

—as one instance among hundreds of others—I need but relate the fact of a travelled Tongan having, some few years before my time in the country, left Niafu in a "whaler," and had seen something of life in other countries, during his wanderings, and had now returned. He informed the King, among other things, that his subjects were being most grossly cheated by the whites residing in the Friendly Islands, and especially in the case of disposing of their pigs. George said that he should be exceedingly obliged to him if he would enlighten him on the subject. The traveller said that the pigs ought to be sold by the joint instead of whole. The King asked if he had a pig of his own. He said that he was the owner of a very large hog, when his Majesty requested, as a favour, that he should kill it, and show the untravelled people, including himself, the way these things were done. The traveller, with all alacrity, butchered the grunter, nicely cleaned it, cut it up into the approved joints, and hawked them round to the whole of the few white settlers at that time in Niafu, but they all said that they did not want any pork just then.

In the afternoon, at a "kava" drinking, this new butcher, among scores of other people, made his

appearance, when George asked him if he had disposed of the joints and what he had realized by the
new method? The native made answer that he had
not, because the whites were a very bad set! "But
have you salted them then?" "No, your Majesty, I
have no salt." "Well then" said his Majesty, "you
had better bring them here, and we will eat them as
'fono' after the grog"—"fono" is a crust after
liquor—"rather than allow them to waste." The
traveller brought them along soon afterwards, together with a proportionate quantity of vegetables,
all nicely cooked, when all was speedily demolished,
amidst a good deal of sly tittering, by these proverbially able trenchermen! "Now," said the King "you
have lost your pig, besides the vegetables and all the
labour of the cooking, and all you get for your
trouble is, that you are heartily laughed at by all
these full-bellied gourmands, and all because you
wished to appear wiser than your neighbours! Did
you not know that if the whites refused to purchase
your joints at a price for which they could buy a
whole pig, that there was no way of compelling them
to do so, and besides, they are much better butchers
than we ourselves are!"

Respecting King George's goodness and generosity. He seldom troubled any of the missionaries for the slightest thing he happened to be in need of, albeit he well knew that they were much better able to afford to oblige him than anyone else in the groups, but rather preferred troubling the smallest of the poor whites, and he generally did this for the sake of rewarding them a hundredfold, nay, in some instances, a thousandfold. I remember one Saturday, just after his arrival from Nukualofa in Tongatabu, in unpacking his travelling case, it was discovered that there was no soap, and wishing to have a shave in readiness for the morrow's Sabbath, he sent one of his people to me for a piece, and with which I, of course, immediately obliged him. On the following Monday morning, about ten o'clock, the same native who had been sent for the soap, came along and presented me with a small paper parcel with the King's compliments. I undid the paper, and here, to my great surprise, was George's *own* gold watch, with a long, massive gold chain attached—a chain which I had myself purchased but a few months previous from Mr. Williams with his own money for him—the price being ninety dollars.

I asked the native, what it meant? when he said, "Do you forget sending the soap the day before yes-

CANNIBAL JACK

terday?" I said, "But the watch and its chain are too valuable for one to think of accepting!" when he made answer by asking "If I wished to run the risk of offending Tuekanokopula by refusing it?"

He was truly the right man in the right place. Yet, notwithstanding his, in some instances, strict rule and wise oversight, these reprobate subjects of his kept him on the constant trot. He kept up continually his regular rounds from group to group, *for years,* and perhaps is doing so now, if alive, and I have every reason to believe he is, first at Nukualofa in Tongalake, then to Lefuka in Hapai, and lastly to Niafu in Vavao. He must be now over ninety years old, and may he live to a hundred or even two hundred if he is happy in this life, for he was really and truly a good man to whites and especially to myself. As for living for ever in a happy state hereafter, that, I think, has been long ago settled, for he was really, according to his light, a pious man, and has preached the Gospel, directing others as far as he was able in the right path, ever since I first knew him—thanks to missionary teaching in the first instance.

THE missionaries had to introduce the chanting form in all the schools, for the children, and especially for the adults, in order to make their lessons somewhat interesting, so as to induce them to learn *something,* and yet it appeared that they had not all improved by the sing-song mode to any remarkable extent, for frequently when I sold pigs to the Yankee skippers whilst counting up the price on the galley door—my piece of chalk versus the "Old Man's" pencil—they would take the figure 3 as the representative of a pig's ear, and the tail of the figure 9 as its tail, and swear in their envy that I was receiving dollars for every individual portion of my pigs, not excluding even ears and tails! But then the Tongans are not as big fools as they pretend to be, for if there is a Hibernian type in the Pacific it is certainly this one!

I sold my pigs wholesale to the American ships —blood, body and bones—for half cash, the rest trash—whenever I was lucky enough to screw this much of the almighty dollar from "Jonathan" and then he would always declare that the "old countryman had considerably shaved him, he guessed!"

I was at this time accumulating money fast, as I had about fifty irons in the fire at once, and not one of them burnt. I supplied as many as thirty or forty ships in the season during the year, with pork and vegetables at quite a thousand per cent. profit. I neglected nothing with which I could make money, not so much for the love of it—as I did not at that time any more than now worship it—as for the amusement it gave me in accumulating it. Even the red chilli-peppers which grew wild all round, I employed the boys and girls to gather them in bushels, and then bottled them up in vinegar which I made myself from the ripe bananas, and sold hundreds of bottles to the foremast hands of all these ships for a half a dollar each when it happened to be money, and if not money, perhaps a "hickery" shirt, worth to me quite two dollars, as I could convert all these things into pigs, which in the end meant money. I bought and begged all the books—new and old— I could lay my hands upon, restitched the old ones, and re-covered them with gaudy covers in the little book-binding press which I had myself made, and then placed them with new titles in my bookshelves, which I had also constructed myself, where they became the general attraction, and not one of these books left those shelves for less than the thousand per cent. profit—in fact, a thousand per cent. was a peculiar law which I had established in my own mind, for all my business transactions, and I always realized it.

Another source of wealth or income was the way I used to receive the officers and crews of the ships when they came on shore for liberty. I always treated them to a picnic or *"al fresco"* meal under the nice shady branches of the tree which stood on the green where I used to spread the good things of the whole island, including my own house and garden, and for which I never charged a cent, and by this practice I made the more, because they always threw down whatever they had brought on shore to pay for their amusements. In this way I filled chests with clothing, cloth, prints, calico, etc., etc., and after being full to repletion with all the good things inside my yard, some of them, in spite of my warnings to the contrary, "guessed they would take a stroll outside and have a look at some of the pretty squaws," and with their "cotton cloth" —*anglice* calico—under their arms they accordingly went.

They had not far to go, for the girls—not being allowed in my house in any great numbers at a time or even my yard, or the boys either, lest they should eat me out of house and home, or otherwise take charge—these as well as all other semi-barbarous people feeling rather too strong when in a crowd to be pleasant—would be waiting for them on the outskirts of the village, according to a preconcerted arrangement with the larrikins, their colleagues and lovers combined. As soon as the Yankees were getting on pretty well *as they thought,* the larrikins would rush out from behind the bushes (where they had been lying in ambush), club in hand, calling aloud, "Oh! you would, would you, make love to my wife, sweetheart or sister"—as the case might be —"and that right before our very faces, would you!" screeching one of those unearthly yells frightening Jonathan out of his very wits as well as spoiling all the fun of his anticipated love-making, and then they would beat a precipitate retreat back to my house, with or without—according to their individual smartness—their *"cotton cloth,"* throwing it to me, saying, "There, stranger, I guess you had better keep that, for I guess these tarnation squaws and skunks don't 'desarve' it as well as you do."

Those of them who had been fleeced altogether, or had dropped their bundle in their fright, and returned with nothing, excepting, perhaps, a good thwack or two across the back from the larrikins' clubs, would tell me that I was more than welcome to it if I could recover it, and which I generally did by the aid of some of the dissatisfied larrikins who had not received their proper share of the booty. I used to intimidate the thief or thieves by threatening to carry it into court by producing, if I could not secure *bona fide* witnesses, bribed witnesses, when it was always returned to me, besides, perhaps, a nice little pig nicely cooked as a silencer. The tills of about a dozen of my large chests were always more or less full of dollars, and I had lots of gold coin besides and no earthly way of spending it excepting in ardent spirits, and which I may as well admit, as I am like the man on oath, supposed to speak the *whole* truth, that I bought pretty large quantities of, sometimes getting fined the usual fifty dollars for landing it.

I used sometimes, after the shipping season was past, when times were comparatively monotonous, to throw handfuls of this money out in a violent passion, scattering it in all directions, and often never recovering it again, cursing it with that degree of exasperation, that any one perceiving me, would

CANNIBAL JACK

have pronounced me stark, staring, raving mad, and
I believe I was, at that time, if not exactly so now,
and all because I could not get a wife in an honourable manner, on account of the then existing prejudice against foreigners, and all kept up by the
constant derogatory remarks of the infernal larrikins—the mildest term for a white man was, that
he was a singed or scalded pig, and yet the ladies
were, as I observed above, physically perfect, and
so there was not in the whole of the three groups
a single female who deserved an honest white man
for a husband, for being weak enough to regard the
hints and slander of these monsters in human form!

I was now the richest man in the place—perhaps
in the whole country—and should certainly have
made a considerable fortune in a few years, and so,
of course, I did not wish to leave, but, to stay without a wife was to me intolerable, and especially as
these tempting ladies were gadding, within sight and
touch too, past me every minute of the day!

I could and would have kept a wife in the grand-
est style—a style equal to that of George's consort
—the queen of all the Tongan Islands, a thing they
were by no means indifferent to, and yet they were
all loth to be the first to break through the *Larrikin*

infatuation? and strike out for themselves, although they all, in secret, coveted most ardently the position!

Maata, my old flame, was *now*, of course, out of the question; but there was another girl who used to come along, bringing me presents, in the shape of eggs, fruit, etc., and her father—a petty chief—observing this, and rather liked the growing intimacy, told me plainly, prejudice aside, that the man who could own a hundred large breeding sows, all in pig, whether he were black or white, red or yellow, should get his sanction for his daughter's hand. I soon had the stipulated number, claimed the father's sanction and received it—mother she had none—and then left it to the lady herself when the nuptials should be celebrated. They were postponed till proper preparations were made. In about a week after this, there was a hue and cry all over the place, that Miss So-and-so had eloped with Master So-and-so—the biggest larrikin in the country! They had taken to the bush, and when found, and which did not happen till after quite a month's search, they each got a twelvemonth—the one to make roads, the other to beat tappa.

There was one good effect those paroxysms of

rage of mine, above mentioned, had, and that was, that the larrikins were thereby rendered exceedingly chary of me, as they were alarmed to the last degree, and well they might be, for I can assure you, sagacious reader, that they were in the most imminent danger! I don't believe that any single one of them could have been induced by the promise of any amount of money, to have ventured into my yard, to say nothing of the house, and as for them coming in a body, why, that would have been the very thing to render me wholly, instead of *partially* mad, consequently desperately dangerous, to them at any rate! It was laughable to see such a number of six-footers rush past my house with such speed—a guilty conscience wanting no accusing!—and yet I had never used any *audible* threats, but then they were legible enough, no doubt, on my countenance! and physiognomy is by no means confined to civilized people!

SOMETIME previous to my residence in Vavao, there had been one or two, if not more, bad missionaries located there. Stare not, good Reader, at this unequivocal statement, because I can assure you, that missionaries, like other people, are composed of good, bad, and indifferent. These gentlemen had framed the laws first, and then the king and chiefs signed and ratified them afterwards. Through these laws, enacted by the most narrow-minded bigots—men of very little or no education and less brains—they had, among the rest of their misdeeds, managed to ruin one poor white for life, by flogging him with a piece of whale-line, with three overhand knots in it, laid on by a powerful savage, winding it round his naked loins and ribs, and the only wonder is, that it did not, there and then, cut the very life clean out of him! This man's name was Robert Stevens, from the county of Suffolk, England, and years afterwards, through this unmerciful cruel flogging, in the care of a *good* missionary— old Mr. Turner, a man at that time close upon eighty years of age, and I believe from all accounts, had always been a man of great humanity—Stevens, no doubt, died under his care.

Captain, afterwards Chevalier, Dillon, because knighted by the French Government for the discovery of the unfortunate Laparon's ship wrecked in Vanikow in the Santa Cruz group, took this rope to England, where it was exposed; but, as Dillon

CANNIBAL JACK

was thought to be somewhat of a reprobate—principally by the *Sanctified*—no notice was taken of the truth.

And then the whites of the island complained to the captain of an English man-of-war, when the first lieutenant standing by asked, how many foreigners there were on the island, and the answer being, that there were some sixty, perhaps, all told, he said, with more truth than politeness, that they were d——d fools for standing for it!

These ridiculous laws were carried to such a pass, that the people going to chapel on Sundays, were often fined or imprisoned for breaking the sabbath —this "sabbath breaking" consisting of breaking inadvertently, a twig from the road-side as they passed along, or purposely breaking a small branch from a shrub to brush the flies from their persons with.

The influence of these culpable proceedings of the former missionaries lasted right up to my time in Vavao, and how long afterwards, I am unable to say—at any rate, it tended very much to degrade all foreigners—some of them quite respectable people— in the eyes of the natives, the policy of such demoralizing aggressions even lowered these respectable ones in their own estimation!

CANNIBAL JACK

Would it be believed that there was one of these former missionaries, in order to establish in the eyes of the natives his superior sanctity, in contrast with all outsiders, whenever he saw a white coming along anywhere about the settlement, that he would immediately bolt off in an opposite direction, calling aloud, *"Here comes the devil!"* And that the natives took up the same cudgels and bolted too. Between missionary and natives they made it that hot for the foreigner, that out of the sixty former residents, when I arrived there were but six left, the very thing his Reverence had been aiming at!

Addenda, or errata:—

1. Instead of "sedan," in my East India travels, read palaquin, because although these two things are nearly identical, yet they have local designations peculiar to each.

2. Instead of "the merciful dictates of the gospel of forbearance," in the description I have given of the conditions whereby the widows could be saved on the Island of Komo, read, the merciful forbearance of the Gospel dictates.

THE END

236

CPSIA information can be obtained
at www.ICGtesting.com
Printed in the USA
LVHW072347070623
749154LV00003B/124